Brick Road
A COLLECTION OF
SHORT STORIES
EDITED BY
ALISON

First published in Great Britain in 2010 by:

YoungWriters

Remus House
Coltsfoot Drive
Peterborough
PE2 9BF
Telephone: 01733 890066
Website: www.youngwriters.co.uk

Book Design by Ali Smith & Tim Christian

SB ISBN 978-0-85739-246-6

Foreword

Since Young Writers was established we have always endeavoured to promote the joys of reading and writing to children and young adults. Nearly two decades on, we remain just as committed to developing and nurturing the creative talents of the next generation, encouraging them to have a sense of confidence in their own abilities.

This collection is the result of our latest competition, Summertime Stories, showcasing the best in imaginative creative writing talent. The young writers have dealt with themes ranging from holidays in the sun to following desert treasure trails and all sorts of inventive characters including ghastly ghouls and pesky pirates.

The strengths of each creative piece ranges from a skilled handling of the written word, to an inspired vision of character and setting. But above all, each page has that all-important spark of imagination, resulting in a glittering collection that will delight the whole family.

Contents

The Creative Writing

Mum Knows Best

It started at 7am on a Saturday morning. My room light went on, what was happening? It wasn't a school day. Realisation dawned … it was the Gala day. Mum had volunteered us to be on the Nursery's float. So not cool!

'It'll be fun,' Mum kept saying, 'Stop moaning.'

At half-past eight we were standing freezing at the pickup point dressed as Dalmatians, (aptly Mum was dressed as Cruella de Vil) and the float was late. Thank goodness I was wearing a mask and no one would recognise me.

After a couple of false starts we were on the move. The parade lasted hours, toilet breaks were a no-go, someone might see me. I hated this!

The atmosphere changed around 1pm, it was tense - judging time! The wait was horrid, but we got a 1st. Fantastic! The pace then picked up, the horses broke into a canter, and that bit was so cool, but over too soon.

Home by 4pm, tired but happy, and I've volunteered for next year, maybe Mum does know best after all!

Ceona Logan (11)

A Happy Holiday On A Hot Island

Alexa, Eliza and Elsie's class got told they would be going on a class summer holiday to Hot Island. They were all very excited, they couldn't wait to go.

Mr Clarkson, their teacher, put them into groups of four. 'Alexa, Eliza, Elsie and Charlie, you will be team one,' he said.

The three girls went, 'Oh no!' Charlie was their worst enemy! How could they stand a whole week with Charlie? Let's find out!

On arrival at the island the teams were given a challenge. Charlie moaned all the time, especially about the seaweed.

'Ew seaweed in my shoe, ew!'

The girls said, 'Live a little Charlie.'

Sandy Beach was hot with deep blue sea. If you stood on the rocks a wonderful view of the island could be seen. Unfortunately Charlie cut her leg on a sharp bramble. Luckily nearby was the herbal plant Spice Drop. Alexa took the plant and squeezed it onto Charlie's leg. Charlie's leg miraculously recovered.

They found a chest of shiny sparkling treasure. On their return to base Mr Clarkson said, 'Very good work girls, that's teamwork!'

The girls are now all best friends thanks to their Hot Island adventure.

Eleanor Campion (9)

Sonny's Dream

Sonny was bored. It was the summer holiday and all his friends were away. Sonny went outside and was playing football on his own. He got really tired and sat down on a sunbed and fell fast asleep.

Sonny found himself in a big white house and on the wall it said: *Please put all your things on the pegs, like hats.* So that's what he did! He took one step at a time and found himself getting smaller every time he walked. Soon Sonny was so tiny he could be on sale as a toy. When he looked up he saw a little door for tiny people so Sonny walked in and saw chocolate everywhere.

Sonny didn't blink because he was so excited he couldn't. Sonny saw pink lollipops that were branches, blue candyfloss as trees, a swimming pool filled with jelly, a climbing frame made out of marshmallows and most of all he saw Big Ben covered in chocolate.

He ran to Big Ben and put his finger on the chocolate and was about to eat it when his mum was shouting, 'Sonny, lunchtime!' He woke up and just laughed.

Rosie Maxine Brandon (9)

Choco Comes Back Home

Once there was a girl called Lucy. She loved animals but she didn't have one of her own. On her birthday she woke up extra early and said, 'Can I have my present?'

'Okay,' said Mum. When she opened it she found a pygmy hedgehog!

'What are you naming it?' asked Mum.

'Umm, I know, Choco,' said Lucy.

When Lucy was at school, Choco got bored and wanted food. Mum was so busy so Choco went out of the window. Soon Mum realised Choco had gone. 'Choco, oh Choco, where are you?' whispered Mum.

Soon Lucy came home. When she went to Choco, she wasn't there.

'Where is she?' cried Lucy.

Meanwhile Choco was hunting for yummy worms and beetles. She hunted on the road and nearly got run over by a car but ran away quickly. *I think I should go in the forest*, thought Choco. She sniffed and sniffed. At last when she had enough she carefully walked on the road.

Lucy was up in her room when Choco went in her cage. Lucy came for a snack when she cried, 'Look at this! Oh Choco, you're back! Mum, keep an eye on her,' screamed Lucy.

'Okay,' said Mum.

Suzune Mishima (7)

The Journey Into Outer Space

There I was at Kennedy Space Centre on Merritt Island ready for the first launch of the project Martian Excursion Mission (MEM). I made sure that the satellite MEM00111 code-named 'Martian' was ready for launch. After a thorough test, we confirmed that it was ready for launch, but the weather wasn't on our side. Just 17 seconds before expected launch time, clouds gathered and it rained so it was delayed for over one and a half hours.

Finally the rain stopped and the clouds disappeared, we launched the Ares 1 rocket with the MEM capsule on the top of it. I was anxious if it would complete its mission successfully or not. The Martian's mission was a one month mission to Mars.

First it would orbit Mars to take high quality photos and to find an interesting place for the next MEM to land. Then it would descend down to Mars to collect rock and soil. Half of it would be analyzed on Mars and half on Earth to see if there was any difference on Mars and on Earth. It was agonizing waiting for the answer, but it came very quickly. The director had told me it was a success.

Izumu Mishima (10)

Untitled

It was the summer holidays; I decided to make a house out of old cardboard. I cut sides of the house, little windows and doors, then stapled it together ready for painting. I took it down to the garden table under the trees. I painted it pink with little blue flowers around the outside.

Mum called, 'Dinner's ready!' I went in to eat dinner.

When I went back outside there were pretty butterflies all over my house. I shouted, 'Mummy, please can I borrow Dad's fishing net?'

Mum said yes. I caught all the butterflies in the net straight into a jar to show Mum.

'Oh they are lovely,' said Mum. I was so happy.

I went back into the garden, there were more butterflies. I caught them all, took them inside so I could have a closer look. I couldn't believe my eyes, they were all fairies! They were hungry so I gave them some bread. They were so thankful; they gave me some pixie dust so I could fly around the house.

It started getting dark, the fairies said, 'Bye Amie, we have to go now.'

They always visit me every week; we are the best of friends!

Amie Green (10)

My Holidays In Cornwall

My name is Rachel Foster on my exciting holiday on a sandy wet beach in Cornwall. The waves bash against the grey rocks and behind the grey rocks are rock pools. In the shiny water there are different types of fish like starfish, jellyfish and crabs and lots more.

My mum and dad are sunbathing on the hot sunny beach; me and my sister are digging a very big hole in the golden sand.

After that me and my sister make a sandcastle in the wet and dry sand because I get two buckets of sea water but, instead of getting just water, I get a fish! In the fishing net I take a photo of the fish. I cover my mum's feet using a spade with golden sand.

Then we go back to the campsite to the tent and I go swimming in the deep end because me and my sister are very good swimmers. Then after that we have tea and play bat and ball with Mum's smelly socks! Then we play a game of cards in the tent for the rest of the day. That is my day on holiday.

Rachel Foster (7)

Stranded

Tick-tock, tick-tock, tick-tock went the second hand on the clock as Mrs Jones nattered on about keeping safe over the summer holidays. I'm surprised I was even listening over the excitement of six glorious weeks under the hot, beaming sun. Only five more minutes till the end of school and the start of the best summer ever! We were going on a Mediterranean cruise!

Who would have thought a cruise could be so boring! Nothing to do but sit, swim and eat. Boring! Just as we were going to swim (again) a steward came up and asked if we wanted to have a tour. Mum decided we should go. It sounded better than swimming.

The tour included the lifeboats. Much more interesting. The guide showed us the survival kit. It had enough stuff in it to look after a person for two weeks! I was busy nosing at the kit when I realised the others had left. Rushing after them, I tripped, walloping my head on the control panel. I collapsed on the floor.

I awoke to the sound of waves. It was dark and very, very quiet. The cruise ship was gone, I was all alone!

Jemma Kightley (10)

The Castle

Startled by a sudden cold breeze that brushed past me, I noticed in the misty distance a faint carriage made of skeleton bones, swiftly progressing along. Where was it going? What was it doing? I just had to investigate …

Curiously poking my head through a hole in the undergrowth, I saw pointed turrets of a magnificent ancient castle and as I sneaked cautiously closer I saw it was in ruins.

Stone medieval walls as cold as ice were crumbling, cracking and covered in ivy, and a gnarled tree glided up the ruins. It was definitely not in its prime. I crossed the drawbridge over the long-dry moat and approached the doorway, which was protected by a tower on each side. The portcullis rose slowly on its creaking pulleys, the heavy wooden doors swung open and I found myself in the courtyard.

Who was welcoming me into this ancient world? Where was the carriage? I looked around me, bewildered, and turned back to leave the way I had come. Suddenly a ghostly shadow blocked my path. I felt a sudden cold breeze across my cheek again and the portcullis slammed down with an almighty bang! I was trapped ...

Emma Rackstraw (11)

The Day I Got To See My Life From A New World

It was a normal day at my house. I had nothing to do, so was watching television. One of my cats came bolting downstairs, I went upstairs to investigate. There was nothing there but a loud sucking noise coming from the bathroom. I went in and like a giant vacuum I was sucked into a massive spiralling portal.

I was OK but where was I? It was like I'd fallen asleep and woken up in a black, enclosed room.

A massive flash of white light burnt my eyes but it went black again then I was falling like a feather, getting heavier until I was unimaginably heavy. Then I stopped and I felt like I was a feather again but I was soaring through the sky like a bird. I called out … As I did I was standing in my house! What was going on? Then I saw my mum coming downstairs. I tried to get her attention but I couldn't. I was looking around when I realised, I was looking at the world where I didn't exist. *Bang!* Where was I, was I dreaming?

Apparently so …

Kieran Tatman (11)

Captain's Treasure

A long time ago there was a secret place.

One day a little boy saw a book called 'The Captain's Treasure.' He didn't like it much and stamped on it. Suddenly he was changing into a new world. The book came with him. He read it then some other words appeared, it said, 'The only way to get out is to find another book.'

Two dead pirates appeared and a bomb started to blow up. The dead pirates came alive. Then another bomb appeared. He threw the bomb in the pirate's face. It blew up his whole body.

Luckily he found the book. He stamped on it. He never got into the next world. The boy opened the book and it said, 'You need to find a key.' He saw the key on a mountain. There was a trampoline beside the mountain. The boy jumped onto the trampoline and grabbed the key. He went higher and found a door. He put the key into the door's keyhole and started to fall down. He fell into the sand.

The little boy was back home again. The problem was he'd forgotten Mum's book. That meant he was grounded for a week!

Ciaran Mallon (7)

The Little Rabbit

Once upon a time there lived a little rabbit named Millie. Millie had one little secret - she was a magic rabbit.

One bright, sunny day Millie and her family went out for a picnic, and they took some juicy carrots, lettuce and tomatoes.

When they got to the park Millie wanted to play on the swings but the foxes started being very mean indeed and pushed and shoved her. She started to cry until she suddenly remembered her magic. She tried to magic the squirrels to be nice to her but although I said Millie was a magic rabbit that doesn't mean to say she was good at it. The first time she tried her magic she found herself not in the park but in a tall tower face to face with a fox! The second time she tried to get out and ended up doing karate. Finally she tried to magic some food but instead ended up tying up the poor fox.

At the very end Fox was so hurt he ended up magicing Millie home just to get rid of her and that's when Millie realised her first lesson - every magic is good magic.

Danita McIntyre (7)

Tick-Tock

A normal summer's day, two weeks after going away, I hear a bang, I hear a clatter, but when the TV's on it didn't matter. Then I realise the noise is in my head and my body becomes as hot as burning lead. I hear the tormenting sound of the dreaded tick-tock. Counting down to the day when I have to go to school.

Then … but only for a moment I feel calm and cool, you don't have to be a fool to be cool.

I say this because in my school to be popular you have to do stupid things that people tell you to do in your life; some just mess about and others for the wrong reasons just want to stand out.

Many children like me, but they are not open about it. I am not popular and I have my own judge, when I make a mistake no one can I know can hold a grudge.

No one liked me at first, they used to call me Barney. If I knew where I am today at that time I would be going barmy.

So back to a normal summer's day, only just two weeks after going away, I see a flash, I hear a bang as usual, the British weather has never heard of summer. As you can see by what I wrote I am just a boy and school is just school. If I think that can be changed I am really a fool … tick-tock.

Nathanael Rowe (12)

Rivals

Blue eyes clashed with green.

'It's a pleasure to meet you again Mai,' Isabella said politely, picking up her long blue skirt and curtsying.

'The pleasure is mine,' Mai replied, her lazy smirk morphing into a twisted smile.

Pushing away from the tree she was leaning on, Mai grabbed three senbon needles from her belt and with a flick of her wrist sent them flying towards Isabella. Taking three steps to the left, Isabella dodged the needles. Stamping her right foot, a boulder rose into the air and with a wave of her hand she sent it hurtling towards Mai. Waiting until it was only centimetres away; Mai quickly bent over backwards, her hand touching the ground as the boulder skimmed over her and crashed into the tree. Flipping backwards, Mai landed on the boulder in a crouching position.

'Is that all you've got?' she taunted.

'I should be asking you the same question!' Isabella shouted angrily as she pointed a gloved finger at Mai.

Two-all's the score, both girls thought, reaching down for their swords. Who'll win today? Drawing their swords, Mai licked a strand of her red hair before rushing towards her rival. Steel clashed with steel ...

Lucy Milward (14)

Wait, That's Not Possible

The blade swished down. Drat! Dead again. This game was getting boring. Rain or not, I was going to the only place around that was interesting in the rain, the churning stream, which flowed in succession in pools and waterfalls before splashing down to a calmer path.

It was halfway down this, sitting on a moss-covered rock, that I heard the voice. It was thin and pitiable as if it had lost all hope of being heard, and in fact, I was surprised that I had heard it. Looking around there seemed nowhere close that the voice could have come from unless, no, I don't believe it; there was a glimmer of colour behind the gush of water.

Shoving myself through the freezing torrent, I found a fainted girl with an awkwardly-angled ankle. After picking her up, I leapt through the water onto the rock I was previously sitting on.

The cold water woke her, she shuddered, and when she found herself in my arms screamed and pushed away off the edge into the water. I looked down, expecting the worse, but there was nothing there. However, in the undergrowth, I saw a flicker of wings. Wait, wings?

Jessica Underwood (13)

The Old Estate Home

One day in the gleaming, gorgeous sun stood an old wood but this wood wasn't a forest in the middle of nowhere, it was part of the old estate that was once there. Of course, if there is an estate there is always a big house, but where? The road was always very busy because there was a caravan park down the road a bit further on.

One weekend, down in the caravan park, there was a girl called Katie. Katie was quite nosy, so on the Sunday, Katie walked down the track into the forest as she pushed and shoved through the brambles, she saw in front of her, a huge boarded up house with chimney stacks that were unbelievably big. Then she saw one of the boards had come off the building. She squished herself through but then Katie saw a shadow, she was worried, she turned towards the open window then ...

'Argh!'

What happened to Katie? Even I don't know!

Storm Ara Rose (11)

Summer Love!

'Melissa?'

'Yes Mum,' I shouted.

'Come down and see what I've got for you!'

A bundle of excitement sprung through me. I'd been on my summer holidays for one week and nothing exciting had happened, so for my mum to call me to give me something, it was pretty exciting. I ran downstairs as fast as I could and ran into the kitchen where my mum was. She was washing up. As I scanned the kitchen I noticed a bowl of watermelon on the counter, I loved watermelon!

'Yes Mum?'

'You can take the plate of watermelon outside and lie on the hammock seen as it's hot outside!'

'Thanks,' I said miserably. I know she was trying her best to make my holiday something worth having but it just wasn't good enough.

As I lay on the hammock I ate the watermelon greedily. I heard footsteps from next door's garden, walking in the direction of the hammock. I quickly got up and started to wipe myself off with my hand.

'Need some help?' I looked up to find my crush, Jermaine, staring at me with a tissue in his hand. He was so beautiful; maybe I'm in love, just maybe!

Tiya Louise Gordon (13)

My Magic Cupcake

I walked into school carrying a green and yellow iced cupcake with three currants on it. I sat at my desk and Miss Longnose came in. Miss Longnose was a bossy boots. She set us the task of writing poetry and it was so boring that I started to daydream.

I suddenly heard a voice saying, 'Hey, I can smell a stinky smell from someone standing at the front of the classroom!' I couldn't believe my ears. This voice was talking about Miss Longnose and it went on and on saying rude words. Miss Longnose was angry and told me to sit in the corner. This was unfair and I was too shocked to eat my cupcake.

As soon as school was over I rushed to my nan's house and told her all about it.

She said, 'I think you have a magic cupcake. They are very naughty things.' My nan told me to pop the cake in a very hot oven so the icing would melt. I then had to dig a hole in the garden, put the cake in and cover it with earth. I did this and I never heard the cake again.

Poppy Clough (9)

Lucy Bear Gets Left Behind

The cases went into the car. Rosie was in her car seat. But I was still there on the bed. The loud engine roared. She had left me!

Next thing cousin Connie put me in a horrible box, wrote a short note and put me in a big red cylinder-shaped container. Apparently I was on my way back to Rosie - but things were not that easy.

The next time I saw daylight a big fat man put me on a very high shelf and said, 'Some silly girl forgot to put an address on you, sorry, but you will have to stay with me.' Stay with this old man? No chance! I jumped off the shelf, ran out the door and started following the road signs. Once I heard Rosie say she lived on Number 1 Woodlands Crescent so I followed that sign that came to her house.

I jumped through the letter box and found nothing there apart from a sold sign. Oh no! I had just remembered she was due to move to the house opposite - forgetful me. I skipped across the short narrow road and there she was, my dear Rosie. Hooray, I was home!

Tabitha Clough (10)

Summer Romance

Summer, spending days in the sun with my best friends and interesting days with the family. But the only thing missing was the summer romance. My best friends had their days out with their boyfriends but there I was all alone. But that was all going to change when I least expected it.

I met up for a final exciting day out this time to the beach with my best friend, Rebecca, her boyfriend Peter and his friend who I did not know, Daniel.

Eventually when we arrived we headed straight for the amusement park, Rebecca and Peter decided they wanted to go spend some time alone so me and Daniel just smiled and headed for the rides. I wasn't a person for big rides but Daniel coaxed me in, saying he'd hold my hand if I needed it.

After hours of talking and going on rides we finally finished up at the amusement park and headed to the beach.

As the sun set Daniel stopped me, taking my hands, 'Olivia, thank you for an amazing day.' With that he gave me a gentle kiss on the lips. Maybe I would have my romance after all.

Katrina Miles (14)

My Real Family

You may look at my family and think they're OK, you're very wrong. I had to do a book report on them telling the reader who they really were.

Mum first. She's a dragon who roars at me whenever I make just the teeniest mistake and constantly terrifies me.

Then I decided to write about Dad. He's kind of like a rat. No, I'm not being a meanie! He's a very smart, devious kind of person who can always trick me into doing my chores or re-writing my homework.

Next there are my three cousins, I have more but I couldn't fit them into the report. The eldest cousin is a grumpy old person (not in real life, but he acts like it), frowning and moaning all the time. Then there are the two little ones who are the complete opposite, they're like cute little kittens, always smiling and giggling. That makes them almost unique in my family.

Finally on the list is me - a majestic unicorn, with a sparkling rainbow mane and deep pink eyes. For some reason, my mum laughed at that part and said I must be crazy! I don't know why, they're the crazy ones.

Sarah Leeke (11)

The Magical Unicorn

Another scorching day on Sandhot Beach in the year 3010.

'Off for a walk, OK Mum?'

Amber watched the sea getting closer but she still carried on, her feet sinking deeper into the wet sand. She felt bitter cold as the sun was replaced by black clouds. Amber's eyes were dazzled by flashing lights.

'Welcome to Sandhot Fantasy Land.'

'Who said that?'

Surrounded by clicking clams, juggling jellyfish and shimmering starfish, a big blue crab stepped forward. 'I am the sandmonster. Welcome to my sanddungeon,' he snarled. 'When the clock strikes noon you will be turned into one of my sandservants!' Sandcastles marched Amber to a sandcave locking the sanddoor. The sandclock's ticking echoed, tick-tock! Tick-tock!

Suddenly bright lights appeared transforming into … a magical unicorn with a rainbow mane and a golden horn.

'Quickly,' he whispered, pulling her up.

In a flash she stood on Sandhot Beach, a glittering rainbow appearing before her.

'Could that really be the unicorn saying goodbye?'

Amber stopped to hug Snowdrop, her favourite horse.
Winking from rainbow-coloured eyes, he gave a loud, 'neigh!'

Amber winked back.

'Where have you been?'

'Nowhere Mum!'

This was Amber and Snowdrop's secret!

Amber Mellors (11)

The Flying Shed

Once there was a flying shed and it was magic. Inside the magic flying shed it had magic tools. The magic tools were a watering can, a spade, a bucket, a fork and a lawnmower. All of these magic tools came alive.

One day the flying shed went on an adventure. It decided to go to the beach for the day. When they were there the bucket and spade saw a family of sandcastles. There was a mummy, daddy, sister, brother and babysitter on the beach. The bucket and spade sneaked towards the sandcastle family and were going to play with them. The magic tools saw that the bucket and spade were missing and so they started looking everywhere for them.

The magic tools remembered seeing the family of sandcastles and decided to ask them if they knew where the bucket and spade had got to. The mummy and daddy sandcastle told the magic tools that the bucket and spade were playing by the sea with their sandcastle children.

When the magic bucket and spade were found they went back to the flying shed and all the magic tools got inside it. The flying shed took off and started flying over the sea ready for the next adventure.

Megan Sherratt (6)

Dragon Adventure

In the six weeks holidays, I went on an adventure to Rivington with my sister and my grandad. After seeing some horses and sheep, we sat down to have a picnic. Whilst we were eating our picnic Grandad fell asleep. Me and my sister then decided to go and play in the castle.

On entering the castle we found a dragon. At first we were scared of the dragon, but he wasn't scary at all, in fact, he was a very friendly dragon. We started to play and then we jumped up on the dragon's back and went flying all round Rivington. Everyone looked so small from up in the sky, we were having so much fun with our new friend the dragon.

After about an hour of great fun and adventure we decided it was time to go and find our grandad. As we said goodbye to the dragon, we started running towards our grandad to tell him all about what we had just been doing. He was just waking up, he's so lazy.

On the way back to the car we started to tell him all about what we had just done with the dragon. Grandad didn't believe us, but I just told him, 'If you hadn't gone to sleep then you would have been able to see the dragon.'

I can't wait to go back to Rivington on another adventure with my grandad, you never know, maybe he will see the dragon too.

Holly Ozard (7)

The Brave Little Bubble

One day two little children were out playing in their garden blowing bubbles. They blew lots of bubbles but only one made it over the hedge! Once the bubble was over the hedge a dog tried to jump up and catch the little bubble but it floated away.

In the next garden a bird tried to peck the little bubble, but a breeze caught it and blew it into the next garden.

In the next garden a baby clapped her hands around the bubble and the bubble went … *pop!*

Katie Stewart (8)

William's Problem

William was fed up of always being last, his brothers would always get cool stuff long before he did. By the time something else had been released, he was getting hand-me-downs from his brothers. William could only dream of what it might be like being the oldest, he could just imagine the new clothes and toys he would get. William started to formulate a plan to get himself more respect and not be at the bottom of the pile all the time. William's birthday was in one month's time so he gave his mum his wish list.

'Are you sure this is what you want?'

'Positive,' replied Will.

The day of Will's birthday arrived, this was one of the few days his brothers gave him some respect. Will was surrounded by presents from his friends and family. He decided to open his auntie's present first, which happened to be socks.

The rest of the morning was spent opening various presents from Lego horses to a soap elephant but he had one present left from his parents, if this worked he would have respect from his brothers. He went to the kitchen and sitting there was a … a puppy!

Leon Bozianu (11)

Pirates Vs Mafia Of Children

I had nothing to do. I was bored of swimming and making sandcastles. Then I had an idea, I could have a treasure hunt. I climbed up a tree and looked out for any pirates.

After two hours I saw a ship sailing towards me. I hid using my hide-and-seek skills then I started spying on them. They were heading somewhere mysterious. I started to get scared. Then I saw a deep dark cave. The pirates were laughing their heads off; one of them dropped a kitchen knife in a bush. I quickly went near the bush and I took the knife.

They went in empty-handed and came out covered with shimmering gold. They finally saw me; I used my tag skills and ran away. I started swimming, they got a gun so I went underwater. I got shot on the foot! I started to drown then I saw a lamp floating. I got it and scrubbed it and an underwater genie came out of the lamp. I wished that the bullet could come out of my foot. When I looked at my foot it was as good as new. Then I wished that I could be bulletproof.

I swam towards the pirates. The pirates started to get scared and started moving back. I punched the pirates' captain and then everyone ran to me, picked me and chucked me up really high. Before I could fall onto the tree branch I wished that I could land safely.

My third wish was to get a powerful Mafia of children. Boom! All sorts of children were in my Mafia: American, English, Chinese, African, Asian. I commanded all of my Mafia to tie up the pirates. The pirates were running for safety but they weren't enough to escape so all of them got tied up.

I gave my last wish to the genie. He wished that he was a human bus driver. *Booom!*

Khizar Afzal Manda (10)

The Treasure Map

One day I was at home on my PlayStation playing a racing game. But I was bored because I kept losing so I went into the creepy attic and suddenly I saw a huge box. I went over to take a look.

I took the lid off and … there was a small scroll inside. I took the scroll out of the box and opened it. The scroll was a treasure map. I suddenly rushed down the stairs and went to the phone to call my best friends Alex and Josh to tell them I had a treasure map. They rushed over. When I opened the treasure map, it was a map of my garden so we all went into the garden. Then we started to follow the map.

We had to go round the whole garden twice so we did. Then we had to go down the steps so we did. Next we had to take five steps forward and then we had to dig, dig, dig until we found the treasure.

It was two hours later and we were really tired but then we hit something … it was the treasure! We were so happy we shouted for joy!

Megan Carsley (9)

We're All Going On A Summer Holiday!

Jack, Mum and Dad were going on holiday. As usual, Dad took the passports, like a man, whilst carrying all three suitcases, like a man, and puffing and panting as if in the gym.

'Jacket on, darling,' sang Mum cheerily. Jack already had three layers on in the hottest part of the airport and wondered if mum was trying to make him hyperventilate. He rolled his eyes, safely hidden under a brown mop of hair but reluctantly obeyed.

'Have you got the passports dear?' enquired Mum.

'Of course!' Dad answered complacently. 'Told you to let the man take the important stuff,' said Dad pompously in the baggage queue.

'Yes dear,' resigned Mum.

'May I have your passports?' the lady with the reddest, glossiest lipstick asked. Grinning, Dad flipped open his jacket and nonchalantly dug his hand into his inner pocket. Then beaming, Dad tossed his head and began frantically patting his other pockets. Sweat began to trickle down his forehead as he became acutely aware of the eerie silence spiralling around him.

Abruptly, with his broad smile and a dreamy voice like a man he asked, 'Who's got the passports?'

Two heads with penetrating eyes turned to face him, 'You!'

Joel Stanley (11)

Door Number 64

Hi, my name is Phoebe and Ricky is my best mate in the entire world. We do almost everything together. We're both twenty now but in our childhood loads of strange but exciting things happened to us, so strange that they're too hard to believe. The strangest of them all was door number 64! Everyone calls it 64 for short. It's an old, old crooked house. Most people believe it's haunted (probably is). But for some reason Ricky and I went close to it, too close. Us two, we both like a good adventure but this one, not really much of an adventure but more like a petrifying mystery, was life changing. It's pretty scary and will most likely give you goosebumps all over your arms and will make all your hairs on the back of your neck stand on end. But I'll tell you anyway. It all started when ...

We were both studying in my back garden, you know for exams and stuff, when there was an ear-piercing scream from 64. Door number 64! Nobody went near that abandoned house let alone live there!

'Let's go investigate Ricky,' I said.

'Are you sure Phoebe?'

'Yeah, it'll be fun.'

'Hmmm.'

I know that was the most stupid idea I'd had in all my life and I don't know why I had it. I think it was because I was so curious to know who and why someone screamed.

Slowly we walked through the huge iron gates and all the way to the doorstep. My hands were slippery with sweat and my teeth were chattering super fast. When we were at the door we froze with fright.

'Why oh why did I say to come here to investigate? I'm so stupid, stupid, stupid,' I muttered to myself. Bravely I rang the doorbell when, all of a sudden, the door automatically opened.

Bang! The door slammed shut behind us.

'Oh my God Ricky, can you believe this, we're actually inside 64,' I whispered.

'Yeah, we're obviously not dreaming.'

'It feels like we are. I've never ever thought of being inside 64. It feels kinda spooky.'

With legs like jelly we climbed the winding staircase that seemed to lead up to nowhere. It seemed like hours but was in fact a matter of minutes before we got to the top. Then we had to walk across this pitch-black corridor. It was so dark that we had to feel our way through. Once we were on the other side there was a door.

Ricky reached out, held the doorknob then slowly turned it then … *thud!* She kicked the door open and we both screamed. I estimated that we screamed so loud that every volcano in the world erupted, that there were more than 100 earthquakes and that all the ice in the North and South Poles shattered into more than a zillion pieces. Oh the sight, the terrible, terrible sight. It was absolutely horrible, gruesome. I wished and wished we hadn't come here and that none of this had happened.

Whenever I think of that moment I get goosebumps all down my back. I'm not sure if I should tell you what we saw in case you get nightmares or faint on the spot like I nearly did but luckily, didn't. If you're dying to know read on …

Maysa Chunara (11)

The Mysterious Depths Of The Underwater World

As the enemy ship swirled about the black ocean crashing and smashing in the dreadful storm that night, one of Captain Slip's crewmates saw something moving. At first it looked like a seaweed shadow. But no, it was the nightmare of every pirate that had ever lived.

July 4th, 1856 - My Voyage Diary
Suddenly there was a breathtaking gust of wind like a tornado … from up here on the deck of the ship it looked like a never-ending churning wind hole ready to greedily gulp!

The next thing I knew, I was in a bed looking outside at mud blowing mist, no … it was a tornado. I screamed in terror. I also felt curious, not sure why. I yelled at Ben, my friend, 'We have got to get back … ' *Crash! Thud!* 'Argh!'

'Where are we?' someone said, trying to suss out what had happened.

We all started screaming, all except for me and Captain Slip.
I just felt numb and Captain Slip was shouting orders, 'No one move … do not go outside!'

Suddenly there was the most piercing sound. Unbelievably, it was a shadow slipper, one of the underwater world's most deadly creatures.

Christopher Pickford (9)

My Summer Story

It was a sunny day in the summer holidays and I was at the Goodwood Vintage Festival. I was having a great time looking at all the old things.

Later on that day I was looking at the vintage cars and motorbikes. They were fantastic! There were Ford Model Ts, old Cadillacs, Triumph Heralds and old Triumph motorbikes and lots more. I was getting in a car to have a photo taken but suddenly it started moving and I saw lots of colourful lights and then it stopped.

I got out and I turned round and there was a dinosaur, I had time travelled! I ran as fast as I could and at the same time I worked out it was a giganotosaurus and it wanted its lunch!

I ran back to the car and all of a sudden I was being attacked by Romans and Celts. I pressed the horn and I was back at Goodwood. My mum was very angry so I had to stay in my room until dinnertime.

While I had my tasty dinner I explained what had happened; I hope they believed me.

And that was my summer story.

Alfie Allum-Hill (9)

The Treasure Hunt!

On a very sunny day
We were on our way.
To a beautiful land
All covered in sand.
We got there by plane
And it was driving me insane.
Because I couldn't wait to get there
But when we did, all I did was stare.
The island was very beautiful
Not at all dull!
It was as bright as the moon
And prettier than a lagoon.
When we all got together
We sat on chairs made of leather.
The director told us what we were going to do
While we had our dinner, which was hot stew.
For it was our pleasure
To hunt for treasure.
We went to get our maps
And set them on our laps.
Studying them carefully
Using them gracefully.
I was looking around
Without a sound.
Then I found the 'X' mark
Under a bar.
I won! I won!
With the sky covered by the sun.
It was a very sunny day,
The end of an incredible holiday!

Ima Begum (8)

Summer Savings

It all happened when Steven and his friends went to the beach one summer in Spain. Steven and Zac decided to cool off in the sea. But whilst they were swimming, a fearsome wave crashed down on them.

'Zac! Zac!' Steven couldn't see him anywhere. He dived under. What was that? A face? Sand clogged Steven's eyes. There it was again, Steven lashed out but sliced his hand painfully on a rock. He broke the surface for air.

'Help!' he screamed. 'Please hear me,' he prayed.

Back under, the water was turning pink from the blood. He saw a grey flash, a shark! Fear struck him. Suddenly he saw Zac, struggling to breathe; he knew Zac wasn't a strong swimmer. Steven grabbed his arm, a shark zipped past them, they were circling. Soon they would attack. He pulled Zac up towards the light but he was heavy.

Finally they reached the surface. A lifeguard grabbed them and hoisted them ashore. Steven and Zac lay shattered on the beach; gasping for breath. The sea had lost its battle.

After Steven had recovered he received a hero's medal. It was the proudest day of his whole life.

Rosie Perrett (12)

Football

Once upon a time there was a football tournament going on. George, Dan, Ben, Finn and Jack were the Red Devils team. They played four matches; they were awesome in the first two matches and won them. Then it rained and the grass was very slippy. Ben scored a goal but bruised his knee when he jumped and slipped. He got up and kept on playing.

At the end the Red Devils won the cup.

Theo Bozianu (5)

Time Travel

My name is Dave and when I was nine years old a weird thing happened to me. It all started when I was in my attic looking for a fishing rod to go fishing with my dad. I heard a noise coming from a box. I put my hand in the box to see what was making the noise and suddenly *fizz, bang, whizz!*

I wasn't in the attic anymore; I was in some sort of training area. I could hear swords clashing. I heard someone calling my name so I went in that direction. As I was walking I noticed that I was wearing armour and holding a sword in one hand and a shield in the other. I wondered why. I found myself walking under an archway into a big arena, a place which looked like the coliseum. Crowds were cheering and baying for blood. A growl sounded from my left and I turned to face a mighty bear. It snarled, saliva dripped from its teeth.

Suddenly, *fizz, bang, whizz!* I was back in the attic staring at the box and listening to my dad calling to ask if had found the fishing rod.

Dominic Bozianu (9)

The Lost Kitten

My name is Bella; I am a lady kitten who loves to scoff food. My story begins in my backyard.

On Saturday my owners went away for a holiday and left me alone, but then, later on that day, a boy named Kevin came to see me and look after me. He was a family friend, that's what I thought.

On that night I went out, I had to do it, to go exploring around the houses for only the third time in my little life. Before I knew it I was viciously lost and cold. I found myself in a messy garden so I bedded down in a playhouse to go to sleep.

The next morning I woke to a loud scream from a little girl who had found me in her playhouse. This frightened me out of my fur so I ran as quick as my little furry legs could carry me and shot over the fence. I landed on my four white furry feet to look up and see … 'Argh!' A large rampaging dog was running towards me and barking at me. *Woof, woof, woof!*

All of a sudden I heard Kevin calling me and shaking my biscuits but I could not tell which direction it was coming from. By now my furry little tummy was so hungry and I was feeling so weak but I was determined to get home so I dragged my little legs and ran as fast as I could. When I turned around I could see that the dog was luckily on a lead. I then darted through a hole in the fence and luckily found myself back in my own back yard. Kevin scooped me up and gave me a big warm cuddle and took me in to feed me some lovely creamy milk.

That's my story and let's say that I didn't go exploring for quite a few days after.

Kevin Harnell (10)

The Jewel Of The Dragon

One ice-struck night as the moon was shining high in the star-struck sky there was a boy named Lance. His hair was inferno-red and rained down to the back of his neck. His eyes were blue on the left, blank on the right. On that night Lance met Destiny at the deep dark lake of Draco. I know you think I'm talking about fate, I'm not. Destiny is a little girl with hair like a moonlit night and eyes of the deepest green.

Once they gazed into each other's eyes the moon started going blue and white. Lance and Destiny stared up at the moon until they heard an ominous howl.

'What is that?' asked Lance. Destiny just pointed to the lake so Lance went to investigate.

In the middle of the lake was a set of two gem-like eyes the size of a two storey bus. Lance just watched as out of the water arose the biggest head, longest body and the sharpest claws he had ever seen. For in front of his eyes was a giant dragon.

'Lance!' bellowed the dragon. The dragon gave him a jewel. 'Take this for your heart is pure.'

Kyle Stockley-Pollard (12)

The Coral Reef

I took a deep breath and dived into the water. The sudden drop in temperature surprised me but the shock didn't last long. Because below me was a sight too beautiful to describe.

The coral reefs were shimmering below the surface like a rainbow that had sunk below the waves. I swam deeper to discover millions of glittering fish zooming in and out of the multicoloured coral. Seaweed was waving in motion with the current, strange-looking starfish clung to rocks and an octopus hovered over a cluster of shells. It was simply breathtaking.

Several dark shapes glided over my head. I gazed upwards in wonder at the five stingrays flowing through the clear water. They had a kind of magnificent beauty that was both ancient and juvenile. I swam closer to run my palm along one of the ray's backs. It did not swim away, but moved closer to me, as though enjoying the feel of my hand. I smiled.

My air was running low and I didn't have much time left. I took one last look at the stunning scene below me, and then I pulled myself upward and swam towards the light of the surface …

Ruby Hyde (11)

The Banana Boat

Mr Banana Head was out summer shopping. He was looking for something for his holiday, when suddenly he saw the most amazing thing. It was yellow, it was big, it was a bit slimy but it was … wait a minute, it was his wife Mrs Banana Head!

Mr Banana Head said, 'Hello dear.' Mrs Banana Head split some of her banana skin dress in fright.

'I just bought this dress for our holiday,' she replied angrily. 'Now it is ruined.'

'Well, we will have to buy you another one,' said Mr Banana Head.

And that was when they saw it. The greatest thing in banana history - a banana boat. Now they could go anywhere for their holiday!

Katrina Donaldson (11)

A Day In The Life Of Gallo And Dactylus

There were once two dinosaurs called Gallo and Dactylus who lived in a little wooden house at the top of a tree in the middle of the jungle.

One day, they woke up at half-past seven and put on their sunhats because it was already getting hot. They folded up their wings so they could fit through the hole in their house and flew all the way to the lake at the very edge of the jungle.

You might have thought that they would be hot or tired but they were used to the heat and very good at flying. They flew right down into the lake with a splash like ducks sometimes do. They had fun swimming in the cool water and had races and timed each other to see who was the fastest.

Their friend, the mixosaurus, swam up behind them and they said, 'Hello.' They caught a few fish and had a picnic at the side of the lake.

They went home when the sun was setting. They told each other bedtime stories then went to sleep and that was the end of their day.

Joseph de Souza (6)

The First Adventure Of Captain Blue-Hooker And His Crew

It was a warm summer's day as the sails of the Jolly Blue Sailor blew in the warm breeze. The early morning horn went off and Captain Blue-Hooker got out of his bed and stepped onto the deck. As he was about to give the orders he heard someone yell. 'Look Captain! It's Mlap Island! Finally all our work has paid off!'

Captain Blue-hooker was about to call, 'there she is lads' when a cannon shot right through the Jolly Blue Sailor. They were under attack!

Captain Blue-Hooker didn't want to get involved in a fight and they were so close to the island so he yelled, 'Jump!' And the crew did so.

They landed on the sandy beach of Mlap Island and watched as the ship blew up in flames. Captain Blue-Hooker didn't make a sound as he watched his life burn in flames right before him.

Blue-Hooker's best friend was the first to make a sound. 'Let's find the treasure!' he yelled. Everybody looked at him and agreed.

They found the treasure and lived happily ever after (as pirates).

Megan Smith (11)

The Cat Bed On A Hot Summer's Day

A tabby cat was wandering down a street. The cat's name was Lilly. She had gold and yellow fur with white paws. This was no ordinary day because in the middle of the road was a purple cat bed. Lilly was tired so she went to sleep in it.

When Lilly woke up, she was not in a purple bed, she was not in the street, in fact, she didn't know where she was. She thought to herself, *where am I?* She looked around and she saw a black flag with skull and crossbones as menacing as a vicious viper and when she saw that she knew where she was ... she was on a pirate ship!

While she was looking around she saw a fat, ugly, smelly man approach her ... *grab!* The man grabbed Lilly!

She was put in the crow's nest (of the ship) and got scratched by magpies! The petrified animal found the purple bed again and she went to sleep in it in three seconds flat.

When she woke up she was in her blue bed in her house but she could still feel the scratches! Was it a dream or not?

Sean McIlroy (10)

Sunset

It was the summer I went to Barbados that I met Russell. He was dark and mysterious with eyes that looked like a swirling sunset. He was magical. I loved him the moment I met him. I talked to him only once. He would never hurt me though. He told me to take his hand, I did, and he ran fast, taking me into the woods, out onto a field. He told me to look up at the sky.

Just then a burning arrow flew out of nowhere flying past us and hitting a tree. I looked into the forest and saw a pattern of bright fluorescent eyes, more arrows and a growl. He leaned in and kissed me, then grabbed my hand and started to run back. As I looked up a shooting star flew above us, I forgot about the present fight and I stopped.

Suddenly an arrow shot into Russell's back, his eyes went from bright red to dull black and a powerful roar grumbled inside of him.

'I-I love you,' he whispered. 'Run!' I turned and ran off into the night, tears running down my face. I blamed myself for everything.

I decided to forget about Russell. It was only a holiday romance.

Alannah Bysouth-Bell (12)

The Myth Of The Stone Dog

Many, many years ago, the Greek gods were peacefully resting on Mount Olympus. The year had been a wonderful and a calm one, except for a few lightning bolts raged by Zeus (making sure the loyal people of Greece knew who the great god was!)

As the year was coming to an end, it was time to do something different. So all the gods united in Zeus' palace and started talking, even whispering about this and that. After a whole lot of excitement, the final decision was made. The Olympian gods were going to make a statue of the most beautiful dog you could ever imagine! Every single particle was going to be thought about and made with absolute precision. But one god was not allowed to participate in the making of this amazing sculpture. Phthonus was the god of envy and jealousy. He hated the gods for not letting him take part in this event so he was going to take revenge!

After a whole day's work, the gods finally had a chance to admire their creation. It was then that all the gods blew a little of their powers into the stone animal. Now the dog was finished!

When all the gods had left to retire for the night, Phthonus blew into the dog all of his hatred! Now the statue suddenly came to life and its eyes became red and it changed everything in its path to stone! The streets of Greece were now filled with fear and anger, stone statues of brave men and women lay scattered around streets.

When Zeus saw all this he struck the dog with a lightning bolt and the animal fell to the ground into dust!

Zeus could not change the statues back into humans but he did punish Phthonus by sending him out of Greece never to be seen again! Maybe this story is the reason why there are so many statues in Greece!

Sào Soulez Lariviére (11)

The Boy And The Whale

The sun rose up and blazed down upon Charlie, a young boy whose house overlooked the sea. On this particular day Charlie was going kayaking, he loved kayaking. He waded out to the depths and climbed into his kayak.

50 metres off shore he saw shadows in the water … a killer whale leapt out of the water and over the kayak! Charlie was scared; he fell out and sunk like a stone.

He saw a shadow circle him and then nothing. The whale had vanished. Just as Charlie was about to drown, the whale knocked him onto its back. Charlie gasped for air.

He climbed back into his kayak; there was no sign of the whale. Suddenly the whale bit a hole in the bottom of Charlie's kayak, Charlie struggled to stay above the water as his kayak sank. The whale opened its mouth. Its jaws closed around Charlie …

He woke up, it had all been a dream, he had never met the whale. He looked out the window and his eyes were greeted with a spectacular sunrise. A killer whale leapt out of the sea. Charlie's heart pounded with excitement, he left the house and headed for the sea.

Sam Newman (10)

The Adventures Of Joe And The Doctor

2.17pm

Dear Diary

Today is boring and it is the summer holidays. It's stormy so I'll stay in my room. I'd love to travel with the Doctor in his TARDIS. I wish the Doctor could come and brighten up my day. 'Please God, please send the doctor.'

2.31pm

Am I hearing things or is this true? Can I hear the TARDIS? Yes! I run to the TARDIS and see the Doctor.

'Have you seen a shadow walking around?' he asks. I tell him no but might know where it is.

'Here,' I said, pointing at a box. He tells me that he'll take it from here so I run to my room and get my Doctor Who ability cards.

I speed into the garden, into the TARDIS and ask the Doctor, 'Could I come and help you?'

'Fine, but stay here,' he replies.

'No, cos I want to test out my knowledge.'

So he tests me and replies, 'OK.'

We travel to 1901 where London is about to blow up and kill mankind. The Doctor couldn't stop it without sacrificing me.

'See ya,' I sniff tearfully while I died.

'Argh!' I scream. It was just a dream, I didn't like it.

Leto Ferracini (10)

Topsy-Turvy

'Poppy, it's breakfast time,' her mum called with her mouth full of toast. Poppy lived with her mum, dad and her sister Rebecca.

Poppy's mum asked if she could put something in the bin for her. When Poppy opened the bin she saw something shining. As she grabbed it she fell through the bin into a different world. There were fish on trees, houses were in the sky and people walked upside down! Everybody was looking at Poppy. She was different!

Poppy came to some stairs leading to a sky palace and climbed up curiously. At the top there was a bolted door. She knocked carefully and a weird-looking queen came out wearing an upside down dress. In a posh voice she said, 'I am Queen Eihpos.'

Poppy thought, what a strange name, but realised it was topsy-turvy world and Eiphos was Sophie backwards.

Queen Eihpos asked Poppy to do a quest, 'Pick all the fish off the trees, cut them open and grab the gems and place them in the golden statue in my palace.' Then Queen Eihpos said, 'Don't forget to …' but Poppy had already gone.

Poppy completed the quest and she was transported home.

Elle Horsman (9)

Untitled

Down in the deep dark, dark woods was a tent with Harry and Cain inside. They could hear spooky sounds coming from outside, now what to do? Go outside or hide?

They opened up their tent and could see darkness, it was cold ... Harry and Cain went to look for more spooky noises in the deep dark, dark woods. They came across a tree, all green and covered in mould.

Slithering up the green mouldy tree, they could see a snake, long, black and red and as skinny as a rake. *Hiss, hiss, hiss*, then suddenly the snake turned his head and slithered across their feet. They ran and ran and ran into the deep, deep dark woods. A pounding in Harry's chest went *beat, beat, beat*.

Then Cain woke up and realised it was all a dream.

Mum called and said, 'Cain, do you want to go to the woods camping with Harry?'

Cain said, 'Yes, that will be brilliant, dreams are not always what they seem.'

Cain John James (7)

The Sand Trap

Molly was a little girl who lived on an island near Mexico. It was a very small island with only Molly and her parents living there.

She decided to look for some summery flowers. She parted two bushes and saw some bright pink flowers scattered along a beach. Molly had never seen this beach before and was eager with anticipation to explore. First she made a sandcastle, a rather big one.

Molly finished her castle, got up and started to walk; she picked the pink flowers as she went along.

When she had picked all the flowers she turned around to head back down the other way. At that point, she noticed something very strange. There were two sets of footprints. Molly looked around again, no one was there.

She ran back to where she was before and her sandcastle had been crushed. She thought it was the sea but then she saw writing carved into the sand. It appeared gradually as she read: 'Get off our beach or we will bury you alive!' Molly's heart pounded, she screamed and ran, stopping to pick up her flowers. Then she realised she had made a big mistake …

Victoria Greenhalgh (11)

The Story Of Babakoto

Once there was a boy called Koto. He lived in a small wooden house in a village near a big dark rainforest.

One day he went into the forest to find some honey. He looked up into high trees. As he walked along, the mud squelched under his bare feet. In the forest he could hear many birds calling and the indris singing in the distance.

Just then he heard a buzzing noise. He had found a bees' nest. He climbed the tree. Just before he could reach the honey, the swarm of bees saw him. Angry that he was stealing their honey, they attacked! Koto screamed. He forgot how to climb down and fell down.

There was an indri around and having pity on the small boy, caught him and carefully carried him to the ground.

When Koto got back to his village, the villagers were amazed about his story. From then on it became 'fady' (bad luck) for local people to kill an indri. In the Malagasy language they call the indri 'Babakoto' which means 'Father of Koto.'

Katie Marsden (9)

The Day I Stole A Bugatti Veyron Sport

One day I saw a Bugatti Veyron Sport in Tesco's car park so I went to have a look. When I looked inside I saw that the keys were still in the car! Though the keys weren't in the ignition I knew where they were. The window was open, not much but I could reach the keys. I quickly grabbed the keys, put them in the ignition and opened the window completely. I clambered in and drove off.

A policeman saw me and chased after me but he couldn't catch me because I could go at 258 miles per hour. I saw Jeremy Clarkson who stopped me but when I got out my skin fell off - I transformed into the Stig.

I drove off back to Tesco car park to put the car back.

When I got back the car owner was still doing his daily shopping. I texted my friend to say I had turned into the Stig and that I had a new car. I took it home to show them (they thought it was cool).

The next day I pretended it was faulty so I took it back to the car park and left it.

Henry Billany (8)

Summertime Story

Sam scrambled after Molly, his dog, along the loose rocks, surrounded by an everlasting army of giant green henchmen. Molly stopped and sniffed the air, then she trotted off at a steady pace before halting by a slender cave entrance.

Sam glanced at the vague outline of another Alderley Edge cliff in the distance before following Molly into the cave. The thin passage was just wide enough for them to fit through. Sam caught a glimpse of the beaming sun as he looked back. They came to a minute clearing and near the roof of the cave a shabby bird's nest lay on a small ledge. Sam scrambled up the wall and peered over the edge of the nest for a better view where he saw a baby bird. Sam jumped down and stood there, thinking for a minute or two, before running off out of the cave with his dog.

As he adjusted his eyes to the blinding sun, he ran into the ranger's hut and explained about the abandoned bird and went to show him. The ranger was amazed by his discovery and rewarded him by giving his family a year's membership to the National Trust.

Harry George Simpson (10)

Monkey Business

Sam strolled towards the beach to meet her friends. Sam and her friends played volleyball all morning. After lunch her friends fell asleep. Sam grabbed the dinghy and hopped into the sparkly salty sea, soon Sam was asleep.

Sam woke up with a bump, startled; she looked up to see a towering golden palm tree looming over her. Sam climbed out onto the golden sands and spotted a monkey sitting by the palm tree. Sam said, 'Hello.'

'Hello,' replied the monkey, 'Are you OK?'

Sam explained that she had fallen asleep and drifted to the island.

The monkey said, 'I can help. We can build you an oar to get back to the beach.'

'Great!' Sam exclaimed.

Sam and the monkey had great fun making the oar. They cut and carved with the monkey's tools. The monkey explained that he lived on the island to take care of the golden palm tree.

When Sam was ready to leave the island she promised the monkey she would visit again. With the oar and the monkey's direction Sam paddled back to the beach, her friends were awake and were looking for her.

'Where have you been?' they asked.

Sam replied, 'Monkey business.'

Neriece Bridgeman (9)

The Diary Of The Sun's Daughter

Monday

Dear Diary, it's me Summer, the sun's daughter. Today I was walking on the beach on Planet Earth in a place called Jamaica. It is beautiful. I saw coconuts falling, the waves crashing over the rocks. I enjoyed it and I saw Mother doing her job. I said hello quietly. It really is beautiful. Met new friends called Becky, Sally and Joe. They are humans. They understand me and I found out that they are very kind. So it should be OK. You know how Mother gets angry when I talk to humans, she gets crazy and I have to move. Mother always stays in space.

Tuesday

Dear Diary, I'm doing the same thing today, high school and Mother teaching me how to use my powers. I can make a gush of fire go in your face. It is cool, no, I mean hot! Mother's doubling the super training and I have got to do my essay on the North Star. It might sound easy but it isn't, trust me, the North Star is not the greatest of friends with my mother. So I'm going to fail that, great! So from all of that I am very, very tired. Night.

Wednesday

Dear Diary, I went missing this morning, I saw a person crying under a tree but the person was a robber and he nicked my money and phone. I had to use a new power, it is called Shine. It is very difficult so I have to close my eyes and think hard about the shine to make it powerful. It took a while but I ended up back in my room. Quite a stressful day, won't tell Mother.

Thursday

Dear Diary, I have upsetting news, I am moving to a different high school and it is in space. I am boarding the rocket now and I am sad because I am leaving all my human friends at school. The new school is called 'Super High for Supers', it's all Mother's fault, she found out I got robbed and was very upset. So I am stuck going to an academy. Sorry I cannot write to you from the rocket but I think I can write in my new school. Mother thinks I will be safer and happier at the new place, she said it is a privilege and very posh.

Friday
Dear Diary, this school is cool, the kids are like me, some have powers and some have weird mothers. Oh let me rephrase that, 'different' mothers. But I only have one friend, her name is Sparkle. She is bubbly and funny. I have learnt so far how to control and create my powers and I have my own school home where I do my homework, study and live until it is the summer holidays, Easter, Christmas and any other holiday when I go home to Mother.

Saturday
Dear Diary, same things today but I know how to make potions and spells. Our teacher is weird and he is called Mr Mange and he is crazy and I mean crazy! I like my gym coach, Miss Cherry because she gives us sweets if we do a flip or a cool spin correctly. So it was a strange but happy day but the horrible thing is, I have a lot and I mean a lot, of homework to do.

Sunday
Dear Diary, Mother is not well and I must do her job until she recovers so this is the last time I will write to you for a while. Mother's job is very hard and is 24/7. I know this might sound horrible but it's okay, it won't be for long. Miss you, goodbye.

Beth Bell (10)

Penelope's Quest

My mum and I were strolling through the forest until we saw a dazzling white horse. We followed and it led us to a waterfall, I put my hand through the waterfall and it parted. Then a lady emerged, gliding over the lake.

'Penelope, welcome to Cardeemer and welcome back Jane. My name is Queen Harmonica,' said the lady. 'Penelope, you're to go on a quest to retrieve the sacred jewel, Diamond the unicorn will fly you, Crystal the fairy will help and Hagoon, the man on my right, will tell you what you need to know. Any questions?' she asked.

Only a billion, I thought.

'Now get onto Diamond,' she instructed. I did.

As I was about to leave, Mum shouted, 'Good luck.'

We flew to a castle and entering a booming voice said, 'To get the jewel you'll have to kill me!' Fireballs flew in my direction. I dodged and Crystal sprinkled fairy dust on me.

'Wish for something,' Hagoon said and lightning popped into my head. I imagined shooting lighting towards the voice. *Crackle!* A red jewel appeared in my hand. I won. I wished to be back at Cardeemer ...

'Congratulations!' Mum and Queen Harmonica cheered.

Seyi Owoso (10)

My Favourite Thing

One nice sunny day Captain Mustaqeem and his friends were sailing on a shiny ship.

Harry and Joe were using the telescope - they saw something interesting.

Harry said to the Captain, 'What are the pirates doing? They look lost.'

Captain said, 'They all must be looking for the treasure I heard about!'

The sun shone into Peter's eyes, he lost control and hit one of the rocks. The ship landed upside down.

Everyone said, 'Argh!' and other noises came like *whoosh, splash, bang!*

Captain and his friends had no other choice but to swim to an island. Captain Mustaqeem felt something touch his feet. He dipped his head underwater to see what it was and it was a great massive whale looking at him with a big grin!

Captain tried not to panic and spoke to the whale. He said, 'HFTQAIWSWY!'

The whale smiled and nodded his head.

They all sat on the whale's back and went *zoom!* They found an old island and a cave. Inside the cave they found the treasure box. It had gold coins and a gold laptop which made the captain smile as it was his favourite thing.

Mustaqeem Chowdhury (9)

Philipp's 8th Birthday

On the 8th of August 2010, it was a boy named Philipp's 8th birthday party. He had invited some of his friends from school. Lots of people came and he was very happy. His friend Gordon came. He had a great birthday cake; it was a football pitch cake.

His friend played on his Wii and played football outside in the back garden. They played some games, mummies, statue, dance and pirates.

The children and grown-ups enjoyed the food. The children got lots of sweets.

Two of his friends came to Philipp and said, 'This is the best party ever!'

Philipp really enjoyed his party and was happy to see his friend Gordon. Philipp could not wait for his 9th birthday.

Philipp Leslie (8)

Going To The Seaside

One scorching hot day when the sky was blue with no clouds in sight, there was a nine-year-old girl called Maria who was swinging on her swing and she was thinking of what she could do that day. Maria was a very adventurous girl so she loved exploring.

Suddenly she thought of an idea where she could go out. Maria ran into her house and yelled at her mum, 'Can we go to the seaside today Mum? Pleeeaassee!'

Maria's mum had a little think and she said, 'Oh fine, let's go!' Maria and her mum set off to the seaside. Maria was very excited.

When they arrived at the seaside Maria went rushing off onto the beach. The first thing they did was go in the sea because that's all Maria wanted to do. After that Maria went on a donkey.

'This is so much fun!' bellowed Maria.

Maria's mum went in the sea again so Maria went in as well. By the time they shared their happiness they had to go home so Maria's mum drove back home exhausted with Maria snoring in the back of the car.

When they got home they just went to bed.

Hannah Joanne Lewis (10)

The Time Travel Subway

It was a sunny morning when Mum, Dad, my brother Arun and I woke up and set off on the New York subway. We hopped on the train. It was so unusual. It had compartments with comfortable furniture. Shocked, we sat down.

Pop! A tall bearded man appeared. 'Hello, I am the Wizard Marvellous. Welcome to the Time Travel subway.' He looked down at me and noticed I was holding a book about Henry VIII. 'Would you like to go to Tudor Times?'

I nodded. 'Then there we shall go!' We stared, out mouths open.

'But we are going to Central Park!' cried Mum. Too late, the train was already speeding away.

It stopped. We got off to find ourselves in Tudor clothes. A little man appeared, he passed Marvellous a letter. Marvellous read it out. 'You and your companions have been invited to the wedding of King Henry and Catherine Howard.'

When we arrived at the wedding and saw the king and his bride we all bowed. The feast was amazing. The food was scrumptious. The toasts were amusing.

Later, we returned to the subway safely and waved thank you to Marvellous until he was out of sight.

Anisha Mackay (10)

The Dark Gunman

'Stay away from a man with dark clothing, he is nicknamed The Dark Gunman as he has set off on a killing spree and has already killed seven people!'

As the news carried on coming through, a sense of fear slithered down Jack's back. Jack was only eight and could not yet understand what was taking place in this traumatising terror story. Jack's mum slowly moved over and gave him a hug, he could tell that she was just as frightened as he was but she was trying not to show her emotion as it would upset him.

The next day Jack went to the shop, every step his head swayed to the side checking there was nothing wrong. He saw some flowers for one of the victims. He was shaking in fear. Suddenly, around the corner his nightmare faced him …

Ethan Carter (11)

The Time Travelater

The monster chased after Rhiannon with his jaws wide open and …
I woke up from my nightmare in need of water. I went downstairs and opened the kitchen door, when my jaws fell wide open. A metal box was standing in the middle of the floor. I forgot about water and climbed into it. I closed my eyes and opened them again to find myself … in space on what looked like the moon!

I was in my dressing gown when a robot came up to me, 'Wear this!' I took it from him and looked at the label: Material: ashera, Colour: alomha, Made in Jupiter. I put it on. I looked at a signpost: *Welcome to the moon, 3010. Property of Queen Moannah*.

'So I'm in 3010, cool!' I said aloud.

'Oh so you're a time-traveller? Don't speak a word of us to anyone! I'm Queen Moannah. What year do you come from?' a lady sitting on a frozen star asked.

'My name's Rhiannon from 2010,' I said.

'What do you wish?' she said. I wished to go home. I opened my eyes to find myself in the kitchen. Probably a dream, I thought, until I saw the dress.

Emma Sims (10)

Sunday Crab

Lucy and Mark lived on a boat called Tamarisk. It was a big motor cruiser.

Mark woke up early one Sunday morning and shouted, 'Help! Help!' Mark had spotted a crab on the back of the boat. It was not just a big crab, it was a humongous crab.

Then Dad got up and rushed outside to the back of the boat in his pyjamas to see Mark hiding behind one of the deck chairs and a humongous crab marching up and down on the deck.

Dad stood still.

Lucy appeared and shouted, 'Dad, there's a big crab behind you, get the net.' Dad quickly grabbed the net and then caught the crab.

'Wow, Dad,' said everyone. Mum had come up to see what was going on as well.

Then Lucy said, 'That was not just a big crab, that was a humongous crab.'

Dad said, 'Anyone want crab for breakfast?'

Nicola Sims (7)

Amelia And The Peculiar Volcano

People had started disappearing! No one knew where they'd gone. There was a new maze in town. Both Amelia and her friend, Eve, desperately wanted to go around the maze.

One morning, Amelia begged her mum to let Eve and her go around the maze themselves. She reluctantly agreed. Amelia and Eve ran there, paid and started the maze.

In the middle, Eve picked up a leaflet about what to do next. It told them to squeeze the ball on a stick. Amelia squeezed the ball. Suddenly, a mini tornado appeared, it swept them off their feet into a completely different world. They stood by a spectacular volcano.

Just then, Eve spotted people she recognised. They were people who had disappeared last week.

The girls ran over to them. 'Did you do the maze and come here?' she asked.

'Yes,' someone answered.

Just then something caught Amelia's eye. It was a leaflet which she picked up and examined. It said that they could get out by going down the volcano. They gathered everyone together and struggled down the treacherous volcano. The leaflet told them to press a skull. They linked hands and pressed the skull. They were back outside the maze.

Rachel Thomas (10)

My Summertime Story

Lying on the sunny sand about to go for my midday dip in the hot Spanish sea, I put on my snorkel and dived in. There in front of me were two small wiggly, fidgety octopuses. Their names were June and July. We played hopscotch on the seabed and then a contest followed to see who could blow the most bubbles. I obviously lost with them laughing at me gasping for breath.

Suddenly fear came across their faces. Trembling, they shot off as quick as a flash. Out of a huge dark shadow came an enormous jellyfish with stray beady eyes, towering over me. With a thundering roar he bellowed, 'You're not from around these waters, you look nice and meaty and I haven't had my dinner yet!' He chased me deeper and deeper into the sea, the water gushing down my snorkel. I was struggling to breathe, the fiery jellyfish was just about to sting my bum! There was no way out for me ...

Suddenly Mum woke me up with a lovely ice cream! I had been dreaming in the Spanish sun. I will be keeping a careful eye out for jellyfish on my holidays.

Freya May Saddler (10)

The Hunt

As Stormshade prowled through the dense undergrowth, he wondered if he would meet a plump, fleshy pigeon. A familiar scent wafted into his muzzle as he dropped into the hunting crouch, his hackles rising. *Good, he thought, the wind is coming towards me and it doesn't know what's coming to it.*

Soon the ignorant bird was hanging limp in his jaws. By the time that he had got back to his burrow, Stormshade was completely ravenous. Once he had engulfed his succulent meal, Stormshade decided to expand his territory. Out in the forest he began to urinate around the area where the prey was plentiful and meaty.

Now that he had done his business, he stalked back to his den. He needed to rest. Once he had finished changing his bedding he collapsed onto it and fell into a deep slumber.

Once he awoke from his sleep, he noticed the musty scent of a rogue cat nearby. Cautiously, he began to follow the rogue's scent. Whilst trekking through the moist shrubs, he realized he was becoming closer to the enemy. *This is definitely not good*, thought Stormshade ...

Will Whitaker (10)

Summertime Story

It was a hot summer's day. The sun was shining brightly, the grass was green and the bees were buzzing in the colourful flowers. The day made me feel happy and made feel like going on a mystical adventure.

As I walked towards the beach I saw a trail of footsteps in the rugged rocks. I eagerly followed them. They led me to a sandy beach. I looked around and couldn't see who the footsteps belonged to so I went for a swim.

The water was warmed by the summer sun and it made me feel relaxed. I had only done a few strokes when I saw something in front of me. It had brightly coloured fins and large soppy eyes. It was friendly.

'I have lived here for many years and need a friend,' it said.

I felt safe with this beautiful creature and spent my whole summer playing and laughing with it. I named her Sparkle because she sparkled like a crystal and she would come and visit me at night-time also.

It has been twenty years since that day and Sparkle and I are still best friends.

Holly Tinney (9)

The Story Of Simbar And Salem

Simbar the cat and Salem the cat were best of friends.

One day when they were playing a storm came so they ran away to some place dry. But they had a mission getting there.

'Oh no!' exclaimed Salem.

'Let's follow that path,' suggested Simbar. So they did. It came to a lake. There was a small rowing boat and two life jackets.

Starting to row, Simbar yawned, 'I'm tired, can you row Salem?' Soon they were on the other side.

Yet again they followed the path to a tepee.

Salem said, 'Let's stay here and have it as our home.' So they did. But then an Indian came and kicked them out so they kept walking till they came to a city.

While they were there people fed them and pampered them. Then they came to a lovely cottage that was for sale so they bought it. Simbar went out looking for food and Salem made the cottage homey and comfortable.

They got married at a cat church. Salem had kittens. One called Gracie, another Freddie, another Holly. Simbar got a job and they lived happily ever after.

Kayley Amber Prosser (9)

Summer Camp

'Are you sure you have got everything?' Mum said. She's always been the over organised one. She perfectly knows that I would not leave anything. I'm Michaela and this year I'm going to summer camp for the first time with my best friend Chloe.

'OK, OK, before I lock the door, have you got your toothbrush?' Mum questioned.

'Yes Mother, now please, can we go or we are going to be late.'

Mum put my suitcase in the boot and off we went. Mum put the radio on. Half an hour passed and we were finally there. I didn't want to get out of the car straight away. I just wanted to watch everyone who passed by.

'Michaela!' shouted Chloe. I got out of the car and carried my suitcase out of the boot.

'Chloe, I can't wait. This is going to be the best summer ever.' I said bye to Mum and gave her a huge hug. She nearly started crying but she held it in because she knew I don't like seeing her upset.

Chloe and I walked over to a big huddle to sign in. We were assigned rooms, and fortunately me and Chloe were together. And that was the start of the best summer ever!

Jade Willmott (14)

One Sunny But Scary Afternoon

Tom and Dylan were the two sons of Conner and Billi-Jo Smith. Tom had brown hair, brown tanned skin and was posh. Dylan had blonde hair and was also tanned and was posh like his brother.

The rich, famous family were moving house and also moving to a different town. All of their belongings were in their new gold bricked mansion in Hebburn. They moved next door to Ian, Kathy and their son Lee. They were not as rich as the Smith family but they were almost as rich. The Smith family did not know that the house was haunted.

It was their first scary and spooky night in the horrible dark and frightening house. They all went to bed. Tom and Dylan got taken overnight by an ugly ghost.

In the morning Billi-Jo screamed, 'Where are my children?' Conner heard banging in the loft so he went up to see what the noise was and he found Tom and Dylan tied up. So Conner untied them, they packed up all their belongings and left, never to be seen again.

Lee Thompson (10)

The Boy, The Cub And The Beast

All of a sudden there was a howl and a few moments later a heart-wrenching roar. Immediately Sam knew he had to investigate. He pulled on a hoodie, grabbed a torch and crept almost silently down the stairs. He made a run for the woods.

Even with the moon shining brightly above him, Sam couldn't see far so he turned on his torch. He began to make his way through the trees but then he heard a high-pitch yap. He looked around and saw a little wolf cub but then he looked at its body and saw it was part lion. It started to yap wildly.

Sam stumbled backwards and fell over, his torch flying out of his hand. He heard a growl and two purple eyes leapt out of the darkness, its jet-black body followed behind; the cub attacked. Scratching the beast's face ferociously leaving a nasty bloody gash. The beast tried to retaliate but Sam grabbed a stick and hit the beast in the mouth, a sharp fang fell out. The beast grabbed the stick between its teeth but Sam kicked it back a few feet, it groaned and ran back into the night ...

Billy Gradwell-Smith (12)

A Rabbit Story

A few years back in 2010, my sister Rayna and I were driving through the Moron Park in the Lake District. It was about 2am on Sunday. My sister was driving her new car. She had only been driving for two years and only had the car a few days. She wasn't used to handling it. It was dark. The road was surrounded by trees. There were branches and leaves over the top of the road. It was like driving through a tunnel except that the road kept winding back and forth, back and forth. We were going around a corner when my sister screamed, slammed on the brakes and I heard a thump. I had been looking out the side window and didn't know what had happened but I had a bad feeling that we had hit something.

My sister started crying. She kept saying 'I hit it! I hit it! Oh no, I hit it! I'm so sorry.' I tried calming her down but nothing would work. Finally, dreading what I might find, I opened my door and walked around behind the car. On the ground was a rabbit (or as my sister calls them - bunnies). It was lying on its side. It was having convulsions. I didn't see much blood, but I figured it for a goner anyway.

About this point my sister came around the car and saw the rabbit lying on the ground. She started crying her head off. I didn't know what to say or do. I mean what can you say?

For once in my life I was speechless. I put my arm around her and tried to console her. She just kept crying. I didn't know what to do. The rabbit was still suffering. I didn't think it would live, but I didn't have the heart to stop its suffering, especially with my sister watching. I really honestly didn't know what to do. I just stood there with a dumb look on my face trying to think of something to say to console my little sister.

About this time an air of headlights came around the corner. The car was moving fast and I was afraid the driver hadn't seen us because of the trees and the winding roads.

At the last second the driver slammed on the brakes and pulled to a stop behind our car. The driver of the sports car (a woman about thirty years old) got out and asked if we were OK. I tried to explain about the rabbit/bunny, but couldn't find a way to say it without upsetting my sister even more.

The woman walked up and looked where I was standing. She saw the rabbit at my feet. Once again, I tried to find the right words to explain how upset my sister was, but just ended up mumbling something that probably made no sense at all. She bent over and examined the rabbit for a few seconds. I tried to explain that I needed to do something to help put the rabbit out of its misery and that my sister would never forgive herself if we just drove off. Obviously, taking it with us and having it die in the car would also be a mistake. I kept fumbling for words.

The lady stood up and said, 'It's OK, I know what to do.' Before I could ask her what she meant she started walking back towards her car. My sister and I looked at each other …

Iqra Maqsud (12)

Daniella, A Modern Fairy Tale

Once upon a time, a girl called Daniella lived with her stepmother and mean stepsisters, Cindy and Barbie.

One day, Dani asked if she could go to the disco. He mum said no but her sisters could. Cindy and Barbie were so excited, they went shopping immediately.

Dani cried as she waved the girls goodbye.

'I wish I could go to the disco,' she whispered.

'You can,' said her fairy Gok-mother. I'm here to grant your wish!' *Ting!* The loveliest dress appeared!

'Wow,' she gasped, 'I need a limo and some accessories please?'

There were two more tings and a limo appeared full of accessories.

'Wait … shoes?'

Ting! Some gorgeous shoes appeared!

'Be back at midnight,' said the fairy Gok-mother.

Dani met Ben, the basketball captain and they fell in love.

At 11.58pm she ran off but lost her shoe!

'Whose shoe is this?' the paper said the next day.

'I wish it fitted me,' mumbled Barbie. The fairy Gok-mother heard and granted her wish.

Ben appeared at the door, 'Can I see your daughters?' he said. 'I need to see if this shoe fits!' He tried Cindy's foot, too big. He tried Barbie's foot, it fitted! They lived unhappily ever after!

Pippa Newton (11)

Bob Goes To Greenland

Bob didn't know what to do. Where should he go on holiday? Should he go to Turkey where every meal time they ate turkey? Should he go to Hungary where everyone starves? In the end Bob decided to go to Greenland.

When Bob got off the green plane he looked around to see green houses and green people wearing green clothes. When Bob got to his green room he went straight to bed.

When Bob woke up it was morning and his stomach was rumbling so he walked downstairs to the breakfast buffet. Bob enjoyed his breakfast very much.

After breakfast Bob decided to go to the green, green gardens. When he got there he gasped. The garden was shaped like a flower. Each petal had something different in it. It was amazing! Bob sat on one of the many benches.

Suddenly he heard a splash! He looked at the pond and saw a girl splashing. Bob rushed over to help. He jumped in and grabbed the girl then swam over to the bank and climbed out. After this event Bob decided to go back to the hotel and relax.

Anna Jorgensen-Stephens (11)

Camp Nightmare

It was a cold, stormy night. The tent shook in the wind. I couldn't sleep but was too tired to get up. I lay listening as the trees creaked. I was a bit scared.

I got out of bed to wake my cousin but she wasn't there! I walked to the toilet to see if she was there. She wasn't! I went into the woods, she wasn't there either. I heard a screech! I was frozen to the spot. There it was again. I was stuck. Should I go further into the trees or head back?

After another four steps I stopped dead. Another scream! I ran straight back to the tent. I leapt into my cousin's bed. There she was sitting up looking scared. I put my hand on her shoulder and asked, 'Are you hurt?' She shook her head. I bent down my neck close to her mouth; she leaned forward and bit my neck!

I woke up screaming. My cousin, mum and dad dashed in.

'What's up?' my dad shouted.

Feeling stupid, I said, 'Nothing. Just a bad dream.'

We finished our holiday in peace, but I always felt thirsty after that. Thirsty for blood.

Sophie Doherty (10)

Think Before You Bark

'For goodness' sake raucous Raticas, it's only the postman!' Raticas barked at everything ... water running out of the tap, leaves blowing on trees, the radio ... everything and anything!

On Saturday Raticas was getting ready for his morning bark when he spotted the neighbour's cat snooping around his dog flap. He decided to give the cheeky cat the fright of his life. He was going to teach that furball a lesson and with all his hairs standing up straight he gave one mighty bark. The cat freaked out and leapt through the dogflap and landed on the table where Mr Gooseberry was having his breakfast. The terrified cat knocked over the honey which smashed on the floor and sent the milk jug flying into Raticas' bed. Raticas and the cat rattled around spreading honey far and wide. Mr Gooseberry was furious and threw the cat back into the neighbour's garden.

'Get outside you twit and you can stay outside from now on!' Raticas felt very sorry for himself and curled up in his bed. Suddenly he leapt out because his bed was soaked with the spilt milk. From then on Raticas decided to think before he barked.

Alexander Hulton (7)

Tom's Treasure

One cool summer day Tom was bored because he could not find anything to do, there was no park near Weekend Lane in the south of Wales where he had just moved to. He was 12 years old and didn't know anyone; also, he was very shy.

He went exploring in the attic to see if he could find anything as all his things were still not there from his parents' other house. In amongst a load of old portraits he found a map. It was a map of the street he was on and it said the treasure was under a tree in the garden. He thought, *it's something to do*, so he decided to find a shovel and start digging. The shovel hit a hard tree root and it snapped in two so Tom went to the local shop with some money he had and bought a new one and started digging again. He then hit something wooden and he dragged it out. A plaque on it had the same initials as his grandad. Tom opened the chest to find it full to the brim of glittering gold and enormous emeralds! Tom was rich beyond imagination.

Chloé Whitehead (11)

The Most Amazing Holiday!

Dear Diary

I have returned from a fantastic holiday, the best holiday ever! I travelled to Dubai, it was extremely enjoyable! Mum and I went. The views were absolutely stunning but even more spectacular was the beautiful looking beach! For a few moments I even thought I was in paradise! The only sad thing was we only got to stay there for three days.

I had always wanted to travel to Dubai, (the country at the height of luxury!) I now feel like the luckiest girl in the world because I have actually been there!

When I arrived I just wanted to travel all over the place but unluckily Mother said no. I wasn't that sad because I was in the country where I have always dreamt of being.

The following day was the day I was allowed to the beach. It was marvellous. Mum bought me a bubblegum-flavoured ice cream, it was delicious! Later Mum and I decided to go shopping, we both shopped till we dropped!

The next day came fast but regrettably I had to go home. I really wanted to stay but then again Mum did say we can come back another time. Hooray!

Sophia Hussain (11)

Little Red Rapunzel

Once upon a time a little girl lived with her mum and dad in a small cottage on a narrow lane. Her name was Little Red Rapunzel, her mum and dad called her this because she wore a red cloak every time she went out, she was little and she looked like Rapunzel.

One day Little Red Rapunzel's mum asked her to take some cake and some fruit to her auntie who was not very well. Her auntie lived in a house in the woods; she lived at number 50 Rab Road.

Off she skipped.

Suddenly a witch appeared and asked if she wanted to see her wishing well. She pushed Red Rapunzel down the well then she heard a voice, 'You have three wishes.' It was the well! She asked for her auntie to be better then for the witch to be gone, thirdly, to get out of the well.

There was a gust of wind, she went spinning round and landed with a bump. When she opened her eyes she was outside the well. The witch was screaming and disappearing. She heard her auntie, she was all better.

They all enjoyed a lovely picnic.

Daniella Hall (7)

Volcanic Eruption

Jon was walking in a forest in Mexico on a summer's day. Suddenly the volcano that he was walking right under exploded! Jon ran for his life and told everyone he saw what had happened. There were red flames coming from the mountain with amazing colours flying everywhere. The tree next to him was set on fire by the blaze.

Jon saw a car and leapt through the window. He started to drive off in it only to find out that it wasn't very fast so he looked at the badge. It was a Morris Minor, just like his old dad's rust bucket.

Eventually he reached the motorway only to see a gigantic monster crawling out of the volcano. As soon as it got out of the volcano it started to chase the Morris Minor down the motorway. *Thump, thump*, the road shook and trembled. It chased Jon and when it reached him it raised its huge incredible foot and started to lower it down …

Luckily Jon opened the car door and rolled out before the monster had a chance to squash him. Jon ran as fast as his legs could carry him. Sadly, it wasn't enough and consequently that was the end of him.

George Jackson (11)

Emily And The Cat

One day Emily Slink, who worked on a farm, was milking the cows when she heard her mother calling.

When Emily got to the kitchen, a cat was on the table. Just then it talked! Emily was so shocked she darted upstairs to tell her mother but she wasn't anywhere to be found. That was strange because she wasn't downstairs or outside either. Emily realised the cat was her mother!

Emily rushed downstairs and picked up the cat, who was now wailing at the top of its voice. She ran to the vets, the cat in her arms. The vet did an X-ray and found a sweet in the cat's stomach. He didn't believe the cat was Emily's mother but offered to remove the sweet.

'Oh OK,' Emily sighed.

Back at the farm afterwards, the cat acted strangely, clawing at the furniture and curtains. Emily locked it in the bathroom so she could eat her dinner in peace.

'Emily!'

Emily ran to the bathroom to unlock the door and her mother leapt out and hugged her.

'That was a strange sweet I ate!' she cried. Then they went to bed and slept like the living dead.

Polly Bedford (8)

The Secret Island

Once upon a time there lived two girls called Vanessa and Emma. The two girls loved adventures, they longed to discover an island where tulips were blue and sweets grew on trees. They would want to call it Emvessa.

One day they were walking in a forest when they saw a lake and in the middle was a tiny island with four trees on it. They sailed across on a boat. It was blue with a white line.

As they paddled across the clear water they noticed that there was a purple and yellow spinning thing in the middle of the four trees. Soon they were at the island. They found out the spinning thing was a portal!

After a while they jumped in, '1, 2 and 3,' they shouted. As they were going down Vanessa felt like she was hypnotised but happy, Emma felt like she was eating candy and going on a parachute at the same time - it was lovely!

They landed on a soft mattress and then everyone said, 'Master' so they became in charge with their families in Emvessa forever. Luckily tulips were blue and sweets grew on the amazing trees.

Emma Connolly (7)

Time Travelling

There I was … bored stiff playing on my PlayStation 3 playing hide-and-seek and I just didn't know what to do. I sat there shaking my head like mad trying to think what I could do.

Suddenly I had a brainwave! I snuck into my dad's room and snatched all his tools. I went down to the shop and asked for some cardboard. Jackie, the shopkeeper, asked me what I was going to do with all this cardboard and I said, 'Wait and see!'

I sprinted down to my den and lined out all of my tools neatly in front of me. I got my wrench and a couple of bolts and an hour and a half later I was halfway through making my mysterious time machine!

Two hours later my time machine was complete but I needed to put oil and car petrol in it. Luckily enough I looked in my dad's garage and he had some spare in there.

I made myself a special suit that would let me breathe whilst travelling from one dimension to another, then I went into the fridge and got myself some food snacks and treats, then I was finished! I was getting extremely excited, just one more sleep and then I was heading off in my time machine, I wonder where I would end up?

The next morning I got up at 4am, bright and early. I snuck outside and sprinted down to my den, climbed into my time machine and typed in June 1st, 3013. The adventure was about to begin. I sat in my seat and put my belt on and pressed the confirm button.

First there was a rumble, crumble, crash and then a bang! I took my belt off and looked outside. I was amazed to the top of my head at the sight that was in front of my eyes: hover cars, trillions of skyscrapers, fingerprinted doors, like Back to the Future 2!

Now I thought I should have a look at the other planets in our solar system so Mars was the first planet to pop into my mind. I looked on my screen and typed in Mars … Just as before there was a rumble, crumble, crash and a bang!

I opened the door and I imagined there would be aliens but there was just more humans. They were huge and I was as big as their little fingers! I was so frightened so I slammed the door as quick as I could and went to Pluto. It was a good job I'd brought a big hat, gloves and scarf to put on top of my suit as it was freezing on this planet! I thought there would be humans here but to my shock there were big, green, eight-legged aliens all staring at me.

I stumbled to the floor, not being able to speak as I was so scared. One of them grabbed me and shoved me into its huge smelly mouth!

Suddenly I started to scream and to my delight I woke up and I was in my cosy, warm bed … it had all been just a bad dream.

Jack Palmer (10)

Ghostly Goings-On

I just knew that I had put my cream on the table before I went to the bathroom. It wasn't there anymore. Then, late in the day before going out with my friends, I put my purse on the kitchen table while I was counting my money. The next thing I knew, it wasn't there.

I really didn't know what was going on. Maybe it was a ghost. I got really scared. Then, I remembered my parents saying that ghosts didn't exist. I felt relieved, but even more confused.

Afterwards, I decided to tell my mum about the ghostly goings-on. I went to the kitchen where my mum was cooking and Dad was reading the newspaper.

'Mum, I need to tell something. I think there is a ghost in the house. It's making things disappear!' I said sadly. My mum and dad both started laughing.

'Come with me darling,' my mum said as she led me upstairs. She opened the door to my little sister's bedroom. There I saw all my things in the middle of her bed. 'So there really is a ghost in the house,' laughed Mum. 'Your little sister!'

Maryam Ajaz (11)

Mysterious Whale Stalkers

Gradually rising towards the surface, voluminous deep grey figures multiplied instantaneously signalling one another in beautiful song. Atmospheric, majestic ocean waters rippled gently in the mild breeze, a vivid fiery ball of sun blazing overhead. Meanwhile eager whales energetically pursued one another through weak currents, avoiding immense jagged rocks below.

The sprightly whales' speed decreased rapidly as they prostrated against a large rock, followed shortly by a dramatic transformation in the atmosphere, from lively and cheerful to heavy and oppressive. Distant obscure footsteps gradually grew sonorous. Consequently, numerous stern faced men dressed in deep blue suits adorned with zips, strode intimidating towards the shoreline, carelessly flinging down their heaving holdalls revealing an inventory consisting of colossal nets and other various objects.

Instinctively the petrified whales simultaneously lurched retrogressively in a state of terror and daunt. Cunning and sly, mysterious men submerged enormous nets deep into the vast ocean, stalking their prey. Eventually imprisoning an innocent defenceless baby whale, the multiple nets vanished completely from view.

Dejected, sorrowful bold grey eyes peered out from beneath a mass of fabricated net, bidding her loved ones an affectionate farewell, imprisoned for reasons far beyond her extent of knowledge.

Sophia Revett (11)

Frozen Wastelands

A team of eminent scientists are reported missing in Antarctica. They have been missing for five days. A rescue team travel to Antarctica to find them. Scott, Ralph, Edward and James are very experienced rescuers. They arrive at the main research base by helicopter in the midst of a snowstorm which soon clears.

They set off on high powered snow mobiles into the area known as the 'Frozen Wastelands'.

Several hours later they arrived at the camp which had been torn asunder. There was no sign of the scientists. They searched for clues and found the scientists' diary. They were being stalked by a terrifying yeti-like creature with white matted fur, long hooked claws and bloodshot eyes. With trepidation, they settled down for the night.

Hours later they were awoken by a blood-curdling cry and eerie shuffling noises. They were petrified. They radioed an SOS as a menacing shadow appeared over their tent.

The next day another rescue team arrived at the camp. There was no sign of the previous rescue team. The blood splattered pages of a diary rustled in the freezing breeze and held the only clue to the mysterious creature of the 'Frozen Wastelands'.

Aaron McClean (10)

Christy Goes To The Shielings

Christy woke up one morning. The black house felt so warm with the heat of the summer sun in her remote village in the Scottish Highlands. She climbed down from the ladder from her bracken bed that she shared with John, Duncan, Archie and Mary. Christy was going to the shielings with her big brothers while her dad was repairing the house.

After some porridge, they headed up the glen. John and Archie drove the cattle, Duncan was the shepherd and Christy carried some food, bedding and a pan.

After five hours, they reached a bit where they had lunch before climbing the steep hill to reach the grazings and shielings on the other side. After some oatcakes and scones, they drove the sheep and cattle along the steep, winding path up the hillside. When John found last year's shieling, he was surprised it was still intact.

Later that evening, after a hearty stew, the children gathered round the fire with all the other families, sang songs and danced while old Fraser played his fiddle. When she heard him play 'The Hen's March to the Midden' she knew for sure it was going to be a wonderful summer!

Kirsty Watt (10)

The Thing

One day in June, I was playing on my trampoline when suddenly something popped out of the water and stared at me. I didn't know what it was. I decided to see where it was going.

I jumped into the loch and followed the thing to a hole at the other side. Suddenly the thing turned around, made a noise and tried to bite me. Then I realised that the thing was an otter. I caught up with it and followed it through a hole on the shore. Inside there was an amazing sight. The otter had six babies with her, all eating a fish. I left them in peace to enjoy their tea.

Lara White (10)

Treasure Map To China

It was the middle of the summer holidays. Me, my brother Luke, my mum and my dad had all just got to America; we were staying for a week.

One day when we were at the pool we noticed something under my mum's sunlounger. It seemed to be some kind of instruction. It had a picture of a fish and under it, a shovel. We struggled to find out what the fish meant but we all knew it was something to do with digging. Suddenly I remembered there was a beach just down the road from our hotel and there were lots of fish there, it must have been the beach.

Later on that day we went down to find out.

When we got to the beach we had been digging for ages and we finally found a toy boat in a bottle. With our quick thinking we ran over to the boat just before it sailed away.

After three hours the boat finally stopped. As we were getting off we noticed the sign said, *well done on it*. So we brought out our shovels and dug until we found the treasure chest and brought it back home to America because we knew we deserved it!

Mhairi Duncan (10)

My Favourite Person

It was the start of my summer holidays and I was bored already. I played on the computer, he played with me. I played football, he played against me. I watched football, he watched it with me. He is my favourite person. I go to sleep at night and he is still with me. He watches over me, he will always be my favourite person.

Jordan Butterworth (10)

My Playful Summer Puppy

Once I lived without my pet, thinking about my cat that died. Then one day my mum and dad looked on the computer at puppies (Golden Retrievers).

We went on holiday for a week with my cousin, auntie and uncle in a static.

We headed back home but firstly met my cousin in Holbeach to choose my puppy. We named her Belle then watched the owner put nail varnish on her back.

We went home and went back in four weeks! When we got there we took Belle into the car and drove her home.

When we got home my friend popped round to see Belle. Now with Belle I've never got time to be bored.

Casey Barker (9)

Expect The Unexpected

I wish I knew my mum better. I've seen her in photos but that's all. My parents split up when I was younger and my dad took me under his wing so that Mum could travel around the world. I have received letters from her on my birthday every year. I have them all together in a special place and every time I read them a tear pricks my eyes.

This year my letter was different. On the envelope were drawings of a mother and a daughter. I opened it slowly and read it. My mum's loopy handwriting with her favourite coloured pen (purple) and her neatly folded pages. Her Coco Chanel perfume. I could see her there and then, touch her but she disappeared! Next I read … 'Be in the poppy field as soon as you get this.'

I dashed to the poppy field. Nothing happened. I fell to the ground crying, the wind whistling around me. I shut down and stared into the distance. Then I saw something move.

'Mum!' She ran towards me. She held me in her arms. We were together at last. Reunited, together … forever completed, my best birthday ever!

Lauren Cookson (11)

The Lost Princess And The Bubble Blowing Dragon

Princess Elise was sleeping when a wicked witch took the princess to a dark, damp cave in the woods.

For six years the princess' family searched for the princess, but they couldn't find her.

One day the prince saw some bubbles in the woods, he wasn't sure where they were coming from so he followed them. They led to a cave and inside the entrance was a huge dragon.

When the dragon was asleep the prince tiptoed into the cave passing the sleeping dragon.

The prince opened a wooden door and he found Princess Elise inside. They tried to escape from the cave but the dragon woke up and chased after them blowing bubbles. The prince and princess made it safely back to the castle.

It wasn't long before the witch came to the castle. The queen threw a bucket of cold water on the witch and she melted and disappeared.

The princess asked the king and queen if she could keep the dragon as a pet and they agreed. They thought the dragon could protect the princess from any harm in the future and they lived happily ever after.

Georgia Ella Carr (7) & Rebecca Tegan Carr (5)

A Birthday Surprise

It was my birthday today. Guess what I got? A pen! I'd asked for a bike and all I got was a silly pen. I was so angry with my parents. At first I thought they were playing a trick on me, and when I asked, they laughed and said, 'No, of course not!' They said it was a very special pen. I stormed upstairs and sat on the bed, sulking. Everything was spoilt. I swallowed back my tears and tried to think of something else. Suddenly, the door opened and in came Mum.

'I'm so sorry sweetheart,' she said, 'I forgot to give you the instructions for the pen.'

'Oh thanks,' I said, looking confused. As Mum left the room, I looked at the piece of paper she'd given me. It said:

Draw with me and you will see
The object become real
Use me three times thoughtfully
On your birthday, that's the deal.

My heart jumped with excitement, could this be true? I drew a bike as carefully as I could and to my amazement, it appeared right in front of me. I was completely overwhelmed. This was going to be the best birthday ever!

Hannah Jesudason (12)

Otis The Cat

My name is Otis, the cat. I belong to a witch called Cornelia. Cornelia tests all her magic spells on me.

One day we were testing a spell to remove nasty warts. Cornelia rubbed the potion onto my fur … bang! I was as small as a mouse. It had worked but when it came to changing me back, it didn't work! The only answer was to get hold of a magic plant called the woobalooba which grows deep in the enchanted forest. So off I set.

It was dark and eerie. I crept along until something caught my eye. It was a huge venomous snake who was very hungry. I ran as fast as I could only to meet a huge black hairy spider guarding the woobalooba. I needed to trick this eight-legged freak.

'Hello Spidey, don't eat me. There is a huge juicy fly over the other side of the forest.'

The spider stared at me. To my relief it scurried away. I grabbed the plant and headed home as fast as I could. Cornelia hugged me and set to work on her spell. With a rub and a bang I was back to normal.

Charlotte Amelia Bradshaw (8)

Holding My Hand

Holding my hand he smiles at me in the dark.
His ocean-blue eyes glistening, his lips about to part.
He squeezes me tight and I know that I'm safe
But then a fearsome look spreads across his face.
His soft hand loosens around mine.
I thought we were but I know we're not fine.
He gasps and slowly falls to the ground,
Why am I hearing a little muffled sound?
His crying of course and probably mine too,
How could this happen to someone as normal as me or you?
Of course he's a cheat and he lied to me all along,
He never really loved me, all he did was wrong.
As his painful cries slowly block out his bleeding,
The hole in his chest suddenly stops heaving
And when his last breaths get thinner and thinner,
I smile and realise, I'm the killer!

Lauren Elizabeth Vosper (12)

The Day I Found The Treasure

It was the second day of the summer holidays and me and my family decided to go to the beach. On the way, me and my brothers were playing eye spy.

The last game we played my brother said, ‘Something beginning with B.’

And I said, ‘Beach,’ so I got to play with the frisbee first.

We finally arrived at the beach. Me and my smallest brother played with the frisbee. My brother threw it so hard it landed on something rock hard. I dug it up and I found a chest. My mum ran over to see what was going on. We told Mum what happened and then she decided to open it.

When we opened it inside was just a pile of papers. It said that the chest belonged to a fierce, mighty and old man. It was a pirate called Captain Yellowbelly!

I gave the chest to the National British Museum. In return they gave me £1,000,000. Also I found out that the pirocoligues were after it, the chest! For one extra reward they gave me a shopping spree. For my brother they gave him a complete set of Ben 10 accessories!

Madihah Shah (9)

A Spectacular Day Out!

All excited, school holidays. Mum was taking us to the Sealife Centre. I couldn't wait to see all the strange creatures and maybe even a shark!

We set off on our way.

'Mum, are we there yet?' echoed around the car the whole journey.

We arrived, got out of the car and ran inside. We followed the corridors of glass tanks but to our surprise they were all empty! Nothing in them at all. Everyone was wandering around confused including the staff. But the manger decided to take advantage of the situation and clean the tanks whilst they were empty.

One lady climbed into the shark tank to clean the glass when suddenly she jumped with a start and turned looking down at her legs and then froze with fear ... something was in the water with her!

Suddenly a man came running and shouting, 'Get out of the tanks! Quick! The animals are still here!'

Some prankster had put an invisibility potion into the tanks to make everything disappear.

The manager apologised and said if we stayed to help clean up we could hold and touch the creatures and learn more about them. It was fab! I even got to stroke the shark!

Ceyda Ata (10)

The Purple Dragon

Yes! I had just beaten the world champion on my Xbox 360 for racing in my favourite car.

'George!' cried Mum from downstairs.

'What?' replied George.

'Please can you walk the dog to the park?'

'Why me?' shouted George.

'Because Dad's at work and I'm doing the washing up.'

'Fine,' George groaned. George took the dog to the park, bored stiff when he kept throwing the tennis ball to the dog.

Suddenly he threw the ball and it landed right next to a purple giant lizard thing.

'Argh! Help me!' George ran as fast as he could back home with the dog pounding behind him.

'That was quick,' said Mum in a surprising voice.

'Quick, come with me Mum!' George pulled on his mum's hand dragging her to the park.

'What is it?' said Mum panting on her knees.

'Look over there!'

'What?' said Mum, 'There's nothing there.'

'What? Can't you see anything?'

'No!'

He went to the doctors but found nothing was wrong with him.

But suddenly when he got home his Xbox 360 was broken. He was really upset. The dragon then appeared and fixed his Xbox 360. The dragon said, 'The only way to make me real is to beat Lewis Hamilton in racing.'

So George tried his hardest. Yes! He did it. He actually beat him. His mum finally saw the dragon and George got to keep him as a pet.

Joseph Morrison (9)

Mystery Man

Daniel looked himself up and down in the mirror. He did not understand why he did not look like any of the other boys in his class. Everybody was small and big whereas he was tall and thin. He wore glasses, they didn't, he had freckles and they didn't. He was left alone on the playground whilst the 'normal' boys played football on the pitch. His dad was like any other guy in Preston and so were his mum and sister.

His mum had said, 'It's because you're special.'

That night whilst Daniel was watching his favourite TV programme, the screen started to go fuzzy. Lightning began to fill the dark cloudy sky with light. He walked towards the window and stared out at the amazing yellow light. There was a knock at the door.

'Can somebody get that!' shouted his mum from upstairs.

Daniel looked at the dark silhouette standing in the doorway.

'Come-come-come in,' whispered Daniel as sweat started to drip down his face.

'Daniel, I am your guardian, I have come here because you are in great need of my help,' said the man as he pulled out a staff from his cloak.

Connor Sadler (11)

Bella The Mistaken Mermaid!

It was a sunny day and Bella was getting ready for school but this was no ordinary school, it was a boating school. Bella was learning to sail a boat.

But one day, Bella lent towards the water but there was a problem - it wasn't her reflection! It was a weird looking mermaid! Bella was so sure it wasn't her but could she be a mermaid? Bella never thought of that - no, she was pretty sure she wasn't a mermaid!

It turned out a weird sort of mermaid fish swam up to the surface of the water. Bella was so glad it wasn't her so Bella sailed back to school and told everyone about her amazing trip.

Lois Molloy (11)

Beasts

An orphan boy named Sparky was on his summer holidays and it just so happened he was going to camp.

When he got to camp he went for a walk into the forest, when a lightning bolt hit him and he blacked out. Tick-tock, tick-tock. Sparky hovered away from camp and further into the forest. Sparky's camp mates heard the thunder and looked for him.

When they found him they gave him first aid but he did not wake up. Sparky's body was now made from pure energy sent out a signal all over the globe.

That night a beast came, it was Blaze - the fire dragon.

In the morning Sparky woke up. Josh, who was his best friend and also a fellow camper, told him that the tents had been burnt down by a fire dragon.

Just then Blaze emerged from the shadows and Josh said, 'That was the dragon which destroyed our tents!'

Sparky knew that he would have to battle the beast and so he made a force field shield and sword. He held the shield with his left hand and the sword in his right hand; he went forward as the Sparky vs Blaze battle began.

Just then from the over the beast's head came an evil wizard by the name of Darkagon and he said, 'You will never get his magic collar off!'

Sparky had not seen the gold and diamond encrusted collar around the beast's neck and so Sparky said, 'What collar?'

Darkagon replied, 'The one around his neck that frees all beasts. Ooo! I was not meant to tell you that!'

'Thanks,' said Sparky.

Darkagon kept shooting magic fireballs at Blaze who then shot them at Sparky. Darkagon shot evil magic at Sparky. Sparky was protected as the fire and evil magic were reflected by his energy shield back up to Blaze's collar and it broke the catch and the spell was broken. Blaze was free from the evil curse of the collar and became Sparky's trusty companion. Darkagon fled to curse the next beast.

Ben Edwards (9)

The Falling Tower Of Pisa

One night in Pisa there was a big loud noise which woke everyone up. The mayor said there would be a meeting at 11am in the morning at the town hall.

The next day nearly everyone went to the town hall to discuss what had happened.

'What happened last night? Someone should know,' said the mayor.

Suddenly a man came rushing in and said, 'I know what happened. An asteroid from space knocked down the Leaning Tower of Pisa!'

'Really?' said the mayor.

'Yes, come and look,' said the man.

Everyone gasped. 'How will we put the tower in its proper position?' said a lady.

'We will use the mega crane, someone go and get it,' said the mayor.

A man brought the crane to the tower and pushed and pushed and did it.

'Yes, problem solved,' cheered a boy.

'What about the asteroid? What will we do?' said a woman.

'We will use the statos 2-12,' said the mayor.

The rocket was an automatic so it zoomed to the asteroid, picked it up then in three, two, one, it blasted off!

Esha Shah (8)

The Mysterious Ballet Teacher

I disappeared six weeks ago - she told me not to tell anyone until six weeks passed.

Six weeks before ...

I was sitting in the car annoyed. It was the start of the holiday and we were moving house. Dad had got a job and even worse my sister got to pick a club to pass time and she picked ballet.

A few days later I was changing into my tutu, we went through the rules of boring ballet. I was suspicious about the teacher though, she reminded me of a fairy.

And then one day I asked her and then suddenly a booming voice said, 'You have discovered my secret, bring me your most precious possession or die!'

I thought about it for days but the fairy did not tell me how long I had.

A few weeks later she came to me and asked me whether I wanted to die. I shakily said no and she laughed and laughed. When I asked her why, she said, 'Fooled you!' She was a fairy but the booming voice was a joke.

And that's the story about my holidays. Now I get to go skateboarding. I also wrote about what had happened. The holidays that I thought would be boring turned out to be the best ever!

Umairah Malik (10)

I-Scream!

I'll never forget that night. An uncomfortable hot summer's night. The most unexplained but yet terrifying thing happened. It was like a dream - you know the type, when you can't run fast enough!

An ice cream van at one o'clock in the morning? Dirty and grimy with black smoke spluttering from the exhaust. It was playing a slow haunting tune and then it stopped. Slowly, one by one, the doors of the neighbourhood began to open as children in their pyjamas walked almost mechanically towards the van. The doors of the van swung open and a thin white hand appeared beckoning them in. I stared in disbelief, frozen to the spot. The driver looked in my direction. Swiftly I hid behind the curtain.

Once I felt brave enough I took a quick glance. The van doors closed as I saw the thin cruel face. The van turned round and drove off into the distance playing its eerie tune. Now that is why I hate the summer!

Emily Sample (11)

A Day In The Life Of A Guinea Pig

I wake up hidden beneath the bedding, the newspaper like a warm blanket covering me. I then hear the rustle of paper. I run out of my comfortable little house and watch my owners pour fresh nibbles into my big plastic bowl. I run towards it and scoff down my breakfast. My friends already eating from the veggie bowl which I hate eating from. I just finish off my breakfast and let all my waste out before I have a nap ready for tea later.

My nose twitches as I smell the fresh hay laid out in front of me, once again I scoff down my tea and go back to sleep to start the cycle of a guinea pig again.

Emily Hall (10)

The Ocean

I was in the ocean, the deep, dark blue ocean. I was hanging onto a piece of driftwood but I was also hanging onto my life.

The night before I was in the ocean, I was on the ship called 'The Angel's'. I was in my cabin when suddenly I heard a thud. I went to the top deck to find the boat falling into two! I hung onto the railing for dear life then somebody bumped into me and I was in the ocean.

In a couple of minutes the boat was in smithereens. I found some driftwood and hung onto it then I fell asleep.

So here I am in the middle of the ocean with nowhere to go. Then suddenly the water around me started to bubble! Then something grabbed my foot and dragged me underwater and then after that, well, everything went black.

Rachel McGovern (11)

Lowrie And Maggie's Adventure

Once upon a time there was a girl called Maggie and a boy called Lowrie. They were best friends and they lived in Burra.

They were sitting in Maggie's garden looking at a book about adventures the youth club were organising. They asked their mummies if they could go but both their mummies said they couldn't afford it. Instead their mummies said they would take them to lots of beaches and lots of really cool places.

At one of the beaches they found a cave!

Over the next two weeks they also went hiking up a mountain and camped at the top of the mountain and also at the beach. They made a handy craft stall which make them £50 which they spent on the last youth club trip.

Catherine Williamson (8)

The Lion And The Mouse

One day the mouse was eating nut surprise for his breakfast. After that he met a lion.

Then the poachers came and put a net on the lion. The mouse said he would chew through the net.

The lion said, 'OK'

So the mouse bit the rope and freed the lion.

As the sun went down the poachers came back and found the lion gone. As for the lion and the mouse, they never saw the poachers ever again and they lived happily ever after.

Rose Walsh (9)

Untitled

One day there was a little girl who went to the beach on holiday. Her name was Isabell and she went with her family. She had one sister, two brothers, a mum and a dad. Her brothers were called Jack and Ben and her sister was called Lucy.

At the beach there were hundreds of people. All the people were making their sandcastles out of sand but Isabell and her family were making their sandcastles out of water and sand so it was a bit stronger.

An hour later they won the sandcastle competition! They got a trip to an island with treasure and they had a big party all day long and they lived happily ever after.

Elisha Mumby (7)

Aramispou

The tale of this particular story begins with a brave man or was it a woman? It was difficult to tell as their young smooth face was swathed in cloth. Anyway, as this person ran down the streets of Athens bow in hand, arrows quivering and eyes searching the street like an eagle, they stalked the vampire to its lair, shot it through the heart and disappeared into the night.

As the burning sun rose the next day many men had already breathed their last in the war that was waging in the open fields. Aramispou surveyed all this from the tower window before grimly getting his weapons and setting off to join them. So there Aramispou stood firing off his arrows until he misfired and blinded his one eye (oh did I mention Aramispou only had one eye?) and so the life of Aramispou came to an end.

Murray Dawson (10)

A Scary Swim

Today started like every other day. I took a morning swim, ate breakfast and made my bed but by the end it was very different. By the way my name is Speedo Banatto, the fastest fish in the ocean and I live near Mexico.

As I swam to the Crab Shell Cafe for a smoothie, the water around me turned black. There was panic all around and millions of fish swam past me. We were frightened.

'Swim!' someone screamed. So I turned my fins right around and swam for my life. I went full steam ahead not knowing where I was going. We swam for hours to try and find a safe place.

Finally we reached Coral Cove, the furthest place from our reef - we had made it safe and sound.

'Phew! What was that?' I asked Suzy the squid.

'It was black oil,' she said. 'If we hadn't swum away from our reef then we would have ...' Suzy never finished telling me what would have happened because a seagull dived into the water and took Suzy away. *Well, you can't win them all*, I thought to myself and went to check out my new home.

Ben Hood (9)

Midnight's Scale

Hi, my name is Sapphire, the most fearsome ninja warrior in all of Crete. I have fought terrible beasts and even dragons. But although I've many amazing stories to tell, nothing will ever compare to the day I fought Midnight.

On a cold, misty, early morning, the wind blowing through my long chestnut hair, I stood tall and brave like a war hero. As I set sail on my small wooden boat, a roar shook my eardrum. Slowly drifting towards the horrific sound, waves gushed at me and stung my eyes.

Suddenly, as a wave tipped my boat over, something touched my foot under the salty water which sent a chill down my spine. When an enormous black beast came out of the water, it dived for me. But as I took my sword out, I plunged the sharp blade into its flesh. Midnight gave a howl and sunk slowly into the sea. My sword, however had managed to recover a slimy scale.

Ever since today, it has been my most prized possession and remains a place on my neck. My necklace is proof that I, Sapphire, had slayed the mighty Midnight.

Rianna Hinds (11)

The Adventures Of The Sea

One day I went on my boat. I found a bottle in the corner. I dusted it and I found a note that said, 'To Mr Walker.' I opened it, a beautiful treasure map said, 'Go to three coconut island and put a coconut into a tank of water then in the Ice Cream Cave get a chocolate ice cream, add it to the coconut then dive down in the calm sea and get a gold pearl and mix them together, they will turn into a gold chest.'

So off I sailed and three hours later with the coconut and the ice cream I dived in with my diving suit to get the gold pearl and swam back to my boat. I put them all in the tank and to my surprise, they turned in to a gold treasure chest!

When I opened it I found lots of double chocolate and coconut vanilla ice cream, all for me and then I knew that I was Mr Lucky Walker.

Then I sailed home and I shared all the ice creams with my friends - we were very full up.

Harrison Walker (7)

The Spider Who Thought He Was The Best

One day there was a spider and an ant. They were in a box and the spider said he was much more clever and faster than the ant. They decided to have a race from one end of the box to the other side. This would prove who was right.

All their friends came to see the race. The spider cheated by spraying his web so his legs would not get tired. The spider won the race but because he cheated all their friends said the ant was the winner. The ant was very happy that he won the race and did not cheat like the spider. The spider felt sad that he did not win. Next time the spider would not cheat.

Raees Wint (7)

A Day At The Seaside

One day Mr Parker, Mrs Parker, Lucy, Tom and Matty decided to go to the seaside for the day. Mrs Parker made a delicious picnic; there were sandwiches, crisps, cake, juice, apples and apple pies.
When they got to the seaside it was very hot and the sun was shining brightly.

Lucy, Tom and Matty started to make a sandcastle. They dug a deep moat around the castle and collected smooth stones to decorate it. Then Tom shouted, 'I've broken my spade.' Tom cleared away the sand, he thought it was a rock. He picked up the rock and dropped it into a bucket of water. When he pulled it out it was shining and sparkly. He ran to his mum and dad, he was very excited.

Mr and Mrs Parker said they should take it to the museum. They found out it was a missing piece of some treasure. Tom, Lucy and Matty felt happy and proud that they had helped find the treasure.

Louis Yarnell (7)

A Luxurious Day At Discovery Cove

Stepping onto the white, hot sands of Discovery Cove in Florida, the blistering sun pumps heat rays down upon me. I swelter and am almost drowning in excitement, I slowly sit back on my deckchair, soaking up the sunshine and drinking Fanta. I think of the excitement of actually swimming with dolphins in just five, everlasting minutes. I feel as if time's ticking slowly, feeding me waves of yet more anticipation!

Here it comes! We step into the icily, cold waters, where our little dolphin waits … Soon I will be swimming with a cute, bottle-nosed dolphin named Iggy. I step closer and closer … only two minutes more!

Suddenly the instructor asks if I want to swim with him. I eagerly nod my head and quickly make my way towards another trainer. I grab his fins and Iggy drags me powerfully on an all too short distance. I soon let go. A great tingling sensation captures my whole body, as glittering tears well up in my crystal blue eyes. A wide grin stretched from ear to ear!

I think to myself *I have just swum with a dolphin!*

Zoe Mullen (11)

Potato In Peril!

I was bored, so I went into the woods and I found an awesome hidden spot, so I decided to build a base. Then suddenly I disappeared into non-existence!

I woke up on a small island with a tortoise and a potato. The potato said to me, 'You have been captured by Evil Colin.'

'Who's Evil Colin?' I freaked.

'He's the tortoise and this is his island,' said the potato.

'Oh, okay,' I said.

'Hey you, get me some seaweed,' said Evil Colin.

I walked to the edge of the island where there was some seaweed, I caught some, it was already cooked! When I returned I gave it to Evil Colin and he said, 'Un-cook it!'

What does he mean un-cook it? I thought. I went over to the un-cooking pot and uncooked it and gave to Evil Colin.

'Delicious, time for a tortoise nap,' said Evil Colin.

'Get out of here,' said the potato.

'What about you?' I said.

'I'm his dinner! Rescue me please,' said the potato.

'Let's go,' I said.

We went through the portal, back to the woods and put the spud in the patch. I went home and told everyone about my adventure.

Daniel Cuckow (9)

Dino World

I'm Dan Wexler; I work at Dino World museum. I am moving out next year so I'll need a house. That is why I became an archaeologist. An inspector is coming today, so we closed early.

The inspector arrived about half an hour after we closed, he was little, slender, had freckles and glasses, his hair was well greased. The inspector went round the museum.

After the inspection he hobbled towards the office. I peered through the glass pane. He then sighted my manager, (an ex-wrestler), his eyes bulged at my manager's muscular figure.

'Excuse me, your report.' The inspector shivered, 'You receive 6% to pass, which is roughly a small dinosaur skeleton.'

'What!' my manager growled, spit flying at the inspector's face.
the inspector ran swiftly out of the office.

I went to a field to discover a dinosaur for the next inspection. I discovered a bambiraptor, a dinosaur about a foot tall. I brought it back to the museum and thousands of people came to see it. I received a bonus of £10,000, I was so wealthy I was allowed to take over the museum.

Rahsaan Corbin (10)

The Incredible Save

Walking along the damp, wet pavement, I heard nothing but pitter-patter repeat every second. *Splash!* Stepping into a deep puddle, I got soaked, right up to my knees. The water threatened my body. Looking up in the air, I saw a monstrous castle peering, right before my eyes, known as Windsor Castle, the most enchanted place I have ever known.

Whilst getting onto the tour boat for Windsor - a very special treat for me, I saw a swan ahead, glistening like soft snow. There was something unique about the swan. It was the only bird squawking for the sunlight. I felt misery inside her so badly.

But suddenly, a miracle appeared right before my eyes. As the clouds swam away to the north, the only sight I could see was our golden ball of happiness.

It was most incredible sight of this damp day, especially for my heart and the swan.

Noorulain Arif (9)

Just A Dream

I was walking through a forest, trees swayed back and forth, bushes rustled in the wind, owls tooted as the flew overhead. I was scared, it was getting late and I needed to get home but I was lost.

I saw something behind me, I started to run faster and faster. I came to a stop, panting for air; I could hardly breathe. I was shaking. Then I saw a light behind a cluster of trees, I walked towards it, dodging the trees. It was getting brighter and brighter until it was right in front of me. I forgot about everything; my mind was focused on what was in the light.

Then I began to walk into it. I was not in control of my body anymore and next thing I knew I was in a field where flowers, brighter than the sky, spoke, unicorns grazed under the golden sun and butterflies 20 feet tall flew high in the sky. Brownies sat nibbling on mushrooms and dragons, as red as fire, lay soundlessly sleeping on the grass.

I rubbed my eyes and pinched myself; it wasn't just a dream, it was real!

Jessica Gray (11)

The King Of The Birds

Once upon a time, there was a little girl whose name was Lily. She lived in the coldest land in the north.

When spring came she didn't play with the other children outside, but the birds. She would sing to them, calling, chasing them up and down the ice.

Her best friend was King Gull, he would come down to let her hold him.

When the time came for her to choose a husband she didn't want any of them. She looked out the window.

'Stop playing with the birds,' her father said.

Georgina Ottley (10)

The Magical Dance

One exotic starry night, it was peaceful! A little girl danced on the golden sand and a boy splashed in the sapphire sea. Magical, magical it was, dancing, twirling gracefully. How wonderful for that to be true. Dancing and splashing there on the soft sand and the deep blue sea.

They danced through the night, playing as happy as could be. Laughing, skipping, floating. The dancing went on.

At the first peek of sunlight the children hurried back up through the sand dunes to hide until the moon and stars came out again and the magical dance went on and on …

Eleanor Goode (8)

Rough Waves

In the middle of the deep, blue sea lay a ship, still as a daisy in the sun. On that ship were lots of people, shouting, as they were lost at sea.

The captain shouted, 'We are heading west, through caves to get to the island.'

So off they went on their journey.

It was the middle of the night when they went through the cave - the wind was whistling, thunder moved the ship from side to side. People were crying as rain smashed and crashed on the deck.

The next morning the people were a lot calmer and finally arrived at the island, the sand soft on their feet. Everybody was happy.

Bethany Mann (11)

The Sparkly Water

One day me and my best friends in the world were going down to the beach. We got there, we got ready to go in the sea. When we got in the sea we were splashing in the water.

When we got to the hotel we had a shower.

The next day we went to the beach, when we got there we said, 'Now we'll go in the water.'

A fish came and dolphins. The water was blue. The dolphins came and took me to an island - me and my friends built a house.

Tammy Stout (11)

The Spooks

Once I was sitting in the woods, I came across a house, it was extraordinarily big. I thought someone was still living in it so left it for the next day.

The next morning I had breakfast then I told my mum, 'I'm going into the woods to play. OK?' I wasn't really.

So, I went to the house, I looked inside the window. I saw cobwebs. It was pitch-black so I decided to go inside. I was just about to go up the stairs when I heard footsteps so I hid behind a cabinet. There was a man walking through a wall! He had old clothes and curly hair. I looked into the kitchen, I saw a lady cooking. Then I saw two children playing hide-and-seek.

The next day would be my paper round, I'd come to them last. Their postbox was blocked up so I knocked and a boy answered. He said, 'Do you want to play?'

I said, 'OK.'

Then his sister came out and she said, 'Do you want to play hide-and-seek?'

I said, 'OK.'

I went to hide, then I overheard them saying, 'We will catch him and put him in our soul.'

I started to think what he'd meant. He meant he wanted to become human, so he wanted to put my soul in his so he would come alive.

I ran home!

Ben Brock (8)

Sea Rescue

'Oh no!' shouted Alison. 'There's a big wave coming towards us!'
Jack turned round and spotted a dark blue, rushing wave threatening them.

Jack tried to shout over the wave, 'Let's swim back to shore where Mum and Dad are.'

Alison looked back at the shore just before the wave crashed over their frightened faces. Alison glimpsed Mum and Dad waving frantically, in horror, as their children got dunked under the roaring wave.

Jack spied a sparkling flash of colour on the bottom of the sea, then he felt a strong pair of arms pulling him up.

With Alison next to him, the lifeguard helped them back to shore. As they collapsed on the sand, Mum and Dad flung their arms around them.

Toby, the lifeguard, said with a smile, 'Next time don't go so deep when it's windy, because the waves are too strong.'

'Thanks for saving us,' Alison exclaimed, 'how can we thank you?'

'If you come across my aunty's ruby ring, she lost it yesterday, I'd be very grateful.'

'Hey, I think I saw something when we got dunked under the wave,' said Jack.

'You are very lucky children,' laughed Toby.

Anna Howell (8)

Pirates In The Mediterranean

'Ouch,' winced Lucy as Eric's leg whacked her in the stomach as they landed in a painful heap on the silky sand. The sapphire sky spread out as far as the eye could see, filling the air with warmth from the ball of red-hot fire in the sky.

The magnificent palm trees hung over drunkenly, in thick clumps, although their silhouettes in the sand were that of a beautiful ballet dancer, graceful to perfection.

'Wow,' Lucy breathed, looking around, mesmerised. 'World War II last week, the Vikings yesterday …' she paused, 'but this is the most magical.'

However, this picturesque scene was hastily ruined.

'Har, har, treasure me hearties!' Lucy and Eric quickly took cover behind an enormous rock just beside the shore and looked on with fear in their eyes. A grotesque pirate thumped out of the thick rainforest. Both Lucy and Eric felt belittled by his presence.

'Look what I found,' he roared, dumping a chest on the feathery sand.

'Ah … ah ... atchoo!' sneezed Eric. The pirate spun round like lightning, his enormous finger pointed to the rock where Eric and Lucy were hiding. Lucy and Eric froze as he stormed over …

Emma Taylor (12)

The Nasty Shark

One sunny morning, Adam and Bethan went to a place with lots of sharks, which they didn't know. They thought it was a nice place, until they saw the sharks under the sea.

They went under the sea and they saw the shark was guarding a pearl with lots of magic in.

The magic could save all the animals that were blown up by the dynamite sent by the king to kill all the sharks, but it killed all the nice sea creatures instead.

They went under the water and they tried to get the magic pearl, but the shark was too quick. The shark nearly died, he fainted. They quickly got the shark in sea prison and they grabbed the magic pearl.

They stuck the pearl to a star fish and all the nice sea creatures came back to life and it even saved the king of sea creatures when he nearly died as well. The magic pearl saved the king and queen's daughter, they were very happy to be alive.

Adam Durham (7)

A Summer's Day

The rhythm of the waves and the poppysmic sounds of the sea splashing against the wooden boat lulled me into a dream-like state. A wasp lazily weaved in and out between my fellow passengers, as a warm breeze encompassed me like a blanket. Monastery bells rang in the distance and the screech of seagulls circled above me.

The sun beat down on my face as I squinted at the myriad of coloured smudges on the coastline. The pastel houses like paint on an artist's palette. The sandy beaches were dotted with people. I felt the boat turn. A shadow blocked the sun from my view. A monstrous rock protruded from the waves and beyond it a stretch of sand with many shells scattered amongst the brightly coloured umbrellas.

My feet plunged into the soft sand. I could hear the mellifluous chimes of the ice cream van as it trundled through the cobbled streets. I climbed the winding steps, my ice cream melting in my hands. Perching on a nearby bench, I gazed at the sky. The rich golds and pinks bled into the horizon, staining the sea with its beauty. I sighed contentedly. What a wonderful summer.

Alice Samuel (12)

St George And The Sword

A long time ago, an evil power had taken over the town of Benati. Madness fluttered in the trees; tears swept the nation.

The evil Malavor ruled. Everyone thought that George, his assistant, was his biggest fan, but really he hated him. He only followed him because Malavor had imprisoned his family.

One grey, eerie night, Malavor ordered, 'George, go pack our things, we are leaving!' When George asked where all he got was a stony silence. So they set off, Malavor talking about Benati's sword. They rested in a cave for the night.

The days went on uneventfully. Finally, one hot day they found the Cave of Eternity. Cassandra, our heroine, was already there, sitting silently in a corner.

'Malavor, I was waiting for you. If you want the sword you *must* drink this potion.'

George began to drink for his master. Suddenly the sword appeared in his hands and his body felt big and bold.

He pulled himself to his feet and held out the sword to Malavor. George suddenly thrust the sword - Malavor's skeletal face emptied, the red sky became brilliant blue and the birds sang once more …

Molly Howarth (10)

A Cute And Cuddly Beach Adventure

'Miaow,' piped Willow as she felt the soft, warm, golden sand on her paws. Socks on the other hand was dancing on the sand, trying to catch a butterfly at the same time. She looked a sight, but still cute!

Willow and Socks were two very different, charming kittens. Willow was shy and timid, Socks was adventurous and brave though they both had one thing in common, they were both very cute.

They lived in a town called Poole, both the kittens loved it there.

One day they went on an adventure to the beach, their owners were having a day at the beach and Willow and Socks went with them. John was swimming merrily in the sea, Helen sunbathing and Chloe building a fantastic sandcastle. They were Willow and Socks' owners and they loved them.

Neither kitten had been to the beach before so they went for a little walk. People were whizzing by, the sea was clashing and you could even hear people snoring! They saw a golden treasure chest, Willow gently opened it and inside was kitten food. They gobbled it up. Yum! The cuddly kittens skipped back delightedly.

Chloe Cole (10)

A Fantastic Day About Young Writers

Once upon a time, me - Stephanie, - my family and my chocolate Labrador - Homer ...

'Stephanie, can you do me a favour?' Oh no, it was Mum asking me to do a favour as usual.

Later, as I went to bed I was feeling very proud of myself because I won the story competition and won the laptop!

I heard Big Ben strike, it was midnight. One minute later my bedroom suddenly turned into a beach! The sand was like solid gold, crushed by a hammer and the stones shone like glass. I got out of bed and after walking about two metres I saw a pirate!

'Ahoy there me hearties.' (That means hello). 'You're not going to find the treasure before me.'

'What treasure?' I asked. He gave me a map.

'Here you are,' he said. 'The race will begin in 3, 2, 1, go!'

Homer and I had a plan and we dug a hole together, when the hole was twice as deep as me we found something, a big bone-shaped box. Inside it was full of chocolate biscuits, which we shared with everyone.

Stephanie Rice (10)

It's A Mystery

It was a rainy day in the holidays and I was sitting watching Africa's Lost Eden. I blinked and blinked again as I realised I was sitting next to David Attenborough in the African jungle, watching hippos in the river.

As I looked over my shoulder I saw some elephants heading towards us. Panic stricken we started to run, but where should we go? Into the river with the hippos or sit tight and very still until the herd of elephants has passed? No, we didn't, we headed for the nearest tree and climbed it. We were hanging on for dear life, we then saw a snake hissing at us. What should we do?

Bewildered we looked at each other. We both stared into the jungle, for now we were looking at lions that were looking for food. David and I were their prime target. We were now petrified to the spot, with no way out, we panicked!

The pack of lions were tracking slowly towards us, looking for their next meal. Just as one of the lions clawed at me, we both sat back in my lounge.

Joshua Lonsdale (14)

Jungle Jeep Disaster

It was a nice sunny day to explore. So Mark and his wife, Julia, were going exploring with John, the guide, and his son, James. They were going in the jeep. The steamy hot jungle loomed around them and the trees created shadows with their enormous leaves.

They were driving on the track when suddenly Mark commanded, 'Drive off the track towards those trees.'

'No,' replied John.

'I am paying you for this trip so do it!' shouted Mark.

'Fine,' whispered John.

Then Mark announced, 'Let's go back to the track.'

But John was not listening, he was concentrating on the jeep. It was sinking in the quick sand.

'Jump out!' shouted Mark bravely. 'Now, let's leave the jeep and go back to the track,' said Mark.

'No, we will stay here and wait for help,' said John.

'I am going,' said Mark.

'And I am staying,' said John.

John and James stayed, they set up a camp and got water from the radiator whilst Mark and Julia starved and ran out of water.

Soon they found John and the helicopter found them.

'You might be a business man but you are a baby in the jungle!' said John.

Moral: the moral of the story is that you should do your own job and not interfere with others.

Haya Asad (11)

Platinum In Danger

Hannah woke up feeling very excited because her friend Sophie was coming over to ride with her.

Hannah put her riding gear on, her blue eyes sparkled with excitement as she heard Sophie arriving. The two girls ran down to the stables happily as they went to tack up.

They set off down the leafy lane, their blonde hair fluttering in the breeze.

The girls had been trotting for an hour when they passed some fencing, Platinum suddenly reared up, neighing loudly in pain. Hannah, caught by surprise, fell off Platinum's back and the horse limped away.

Sophie helped Hannah to her feet and Hannah got on Sophie's pony and galloped after Platinum. Thankfully Hannah reappeared leading Platinum, who was limping badly. She inspected Platinum's hoof and saw a nail stuck in it.

Hannah started panicking when suddenly she saw a figure, as it came closer Hannah realised it was the vet!

Hannah said, 'Excuse me, do you think you could help?'

The vet replied, 'Yes, indeed.'

He saw that Platinum had a bad cut, so he took her back to his surgery. The next day a trailer turned up, it was Platinum and she was walking easily.

Hannah went to bed that night feeling very happy.

Tallulah Edwards (8)

My Big Adventure

One day I went to the beach with my family and I went swimming.

When I got back to shore I fell into a hole in the sand and saw a portal. Then I saw loads of cavemen, they tried to chase me so I ran away.

I saw a dinosaur, he said, 'My name is Dino. Jump on my back and I will get you away from the cavemen.' Dino took me to his family of dinosaurs and said, 'This is Josh.'

Josh said, 'Your home is really good, it has a swimming pool and a sofa and beds everywhere in the cave.'

I taught Dino and his family to play baseball with their tails and big hard nuts. They were really brilliant and they scored five runs each. Then they taught me how to hunt for food. They gave me a long branch and vines and a sharp stone. I tied the vines around the stone and stick and made a spear.

I caught a leopard, a lion and an elephant. Then I dragged them to Dino's cave and gave Dino a big surprise for his birthday feast. We all ate lots and they gave me a surprise, a caveman suit and they said I could keep the spear.

I said, 'Goodbye, I have to go now.' I ran as fast as I could to the portal and just made it to the portal before it closed. I went and got out of the sand, were my parents still there or not …?

Lucas Balcombe (7)

Amazing Junk

Lucy, Joy and Zoey were friends. Lucy was ten, Joy thirteen and Zoey fifteen.

One day they went to the junk yard, (they loved junk).

'Hey, look here!' Lucy said excitedly when her eyes spotted a big machine in the middle of the yard. The three girls quickly ran to the centre and took off the big cloth that was on the machine. But when they did they gasped; it was a time machine, it was easy to tell as the biggest clue of all was the big sign on it that said Time Machine.

It took no time till the girls had quickly got in and set the time to the year 2121. Like a flash of lightning they zoomed off to the year 2121.

'Oh, my God!' said Zoey.

'We're in the year 2121,' said Joy.

So for the next twelve days the girls lived in 2121, until one day when a flying car passed by and overheard them saying that they were from the past. An angry mob formed, so they quickly ran to the time machine and went back to 2010.

'Let's never go through time again,' Lucy suggested. Everything was back the way it was!

Sandeep Kaur (10)

The Magic Skipping Rope

One day, in the summer holidays, Lilly went out into the garden to play. As she wanted a toy to play with she went into the shed. When she opened the old shed all she could find was garden tools, until she found a skipping rope underneath an old rake.

Lilly picked up the rope and walked out of the shed. She looked at the old rope and began to skip with it.

Not long after Lilly went into the house to get a drink. When she went into the kitchen she noticed it was different and everything had turned old. The tap was a pump, the table was tiny. Lilly was very confused and walked upstairs, the staircase was old fashioned and so was her bedroom. There was a large dresser, an oak wardrobe and a four-poster bed.

What is going on? she thought and then realised when she skipped forwards with the rope she had gone back in time. Now all she had to do was skip backwards to get back to normal. So she did and told her friends all about her adventure.

Heather Burton (10)

Ocean Adventure

One scorching day, I went rockpooling with my family. The sea was very gentle, however, it had left some interesting things behind. My dad found a starfish and my mum caught a crab!

We had bought a disposable barbecue and I secretly gave some of my food to a dog from a nearby family.

After lunch I went to put the crab and the starfish back into the sea. I was just about to pour the water into a rockpool when I noticed a blue, glowing shell in the centre and as I picked it up it transformed into a snorkel mask! With my mask on I sank into the sea and a burst of colourful life on the coral reef invaded my eyes!

As I got settled a silvery dolphin swam up to me and lifted me off of the sandy ocean bed and took me to the deeper part of the ocean, into a shallow cave.

I saw the starfish my dad had caught, but just then … a bigger, darker shadow drifted towards us. I thought fast. I swam back onto the dolphin and sped past the shark at light speed.

I was delighted when I saw my parents again! On the way home my mum asked me where I had been, so I told her about my underwater fun.

Florence Stanton (10)

Sara's Adventure

Sara was ten years old, she loved to play football. One day she was playing with the football and it landed in a mansion that no one ever went to. Sara was afraid to get her ball as everyone believed that the mansion was haunted. Sara was brave, she decided to get her ball.

The messy garden had snails and slugs everywhere. She gently opened the creaky door which had yucky, green slime and spiders on it. she decided to explore inside. She saw bats, bricks, spider webs and lots of creepy crawlies. There were many rooms, which had broken windows and cages.

One room caught her eye, it looked gloomy. She looked inside and saw a witch. Sara started screaming, the witch woke up and quickly grabbed Sara and captured her.

After a few minutes, Sara remembered the magic key her grandma had given her. The key was special; it could open anything. She got it from her pocket and opened the cage door. Sara slowly crept out of the cage and went down the creepy, rusty stairs and rushed out. She never found her football.

She quickly ran home and from that day on she never went back to the spooky mansion.

Anisha Khaliq (8)

Mystery Of Watson's Bay

Today seemed usual for me and my mates, sat at the beach, eating chips and talking about flying elephants that were better guitar players than Slash.

Suddenly an ear-piercing shriek made all of us bolt upright. All the mothers had a concerned look on their faces and were moving away from the noise.

'What's that?' questioned Mark as all the boys ran in the direction of where the noise was heard.

'It's by the cliff,' I said, trying to hide the fact that I was completely freaked out. At the bottom of the cliff we could make out a girl in tears. We all rushed down to help, but when we got there nothing was there apart from a cold chill down our backs.

'G-g-guys,' Tom said, pointing towards a silhouette moving towards us. The girl screamed again and then it appeared. It was a ghost, completely transparent; its silver teeth would have been shining if it wasn't for the eerie fog that the ghost brought with him. His eyes were grey and hollow, with no emotion. It walked straight through us, absorbing us, draining our energy.

'Get your paper today. Latest headline, four people disappear at Watson's Bay.'

Jack Horsfield (11)

The Lost Ring

Luke stood on the wooden pylon, looking at the sea, thinking he was alone, but he wasn't. He could smell the salty sea; hear the sea crashing on the smooth pebbles on the beach. He felt the strong gusts of wind blowing on his face and rustling his hair.

The spray from the sea he felt going up his leg. Luke watched the gulls picking something up from the beach, then flying into the air, dropping it on the pebbles, trying to crack it. That was when he noticed they were mussels.

Luke started to hunt for mussels and placed them on the wooden pylons to feed the gulls. Luke shivered as he felt the cold waves splashing at his feet. He waded into the sea, because he saw something glittering in the sunlight, so he picked it up as a wave almost washed it back to the sea again.

Luke found it was a mussel and as he was about to throw it onto the stones he saw it still glittered. Luke copied the birds to open the mussel. He went to pick up what was left and found a gold ring.

Could it be the Queen's lost ring?

Max Clark (8)

Strange Goings-On

He died five years ago, Robert Macassey. There were rumours that he was haunting the woods around a hidden house in Kent. It was an old, dilapidated house that was abandoned 54 years ago by an old man. Three years later people heard about the news, so they went to look, to see if it was true, that he was haunting the house.

It took two hours to get there, through the Forest of Freedom. Alice and Ben kept on going up a steep hill, over a wooden stile, along the field filled with cowpats, forever moving forward towards the woods. Alice and Ben soon got to a gate that led into the woods.

'What an amazing walk this has been already,' Ben exclaimed.

'We've got to got through the woods yet silly,' answered Alice.

So Alice and Ben set off through the wood, they saw what appeared to be a big tree, but when they went round the corner they saw hidden bricks under the ivy. Burnt logs, graffiti on the wall, broken glass and a slept-in bed!

What strange goings-on!

Zoë Clark (10)

At The Beach

It was a lovely, hot summer's day. My mum and dad had taken me and my baby brother to the beach. My brother was too young to play with so I was bored. I decided to go and explore the beach. I started to walk towards a cave, it was drawing me in. I was a bit scared but something was making me keep walking.

I came across a trunk, it was very old and shabby looking, so I had a look inside. I couldn't believe my eyes when I opened it and found it was full of treasure. There was a very big ruby sitting right in the middle, glowing, pulling me in to touch it. When I did I felt a funny feeling come over me.

It all of a sudden became very bright in the cave, I turned round to see a little fairy behind me. She told me she was the keeper of the treasure. I promised her I meant no harm, I was just exploring.

Just then I heard my mum calling me, so I asked the fairy could I come back another day, she said, 'Yes, but you must keep me a secret.'

I ran off to my mum, she asked what I had been up to, I just said I had been exploring ...

Katie Fether (10)

The Special Shell

Once upon a time, there was a little mermaid swimming to see the fishes and shells under the sea.

The mermaid was going to a party, it was her friend, Little Fish's birthday. While she was on her way, she found a strange shell, she didn't know that it was magical! But when she put it with some other shells it began to shine and open up. Inside were lots of flowers. The mermaid gave the flowers to Little Fish.

The next day the mermaid was playing with the shell and said, 'I want a beautiful swing, please.' The shell began to shake like a volcano with bright light and suddenly a swing came out! The swing was so nice and pretty. The mermaid said thank you to the shell

The shell said, 'You're welcome.'

The mermaid was so happy that she had a swing.

Every time the mermaid wanted something from the shell she always said please and the shell gave her whatever she wanted, but only if she said please.

All of the mermaid's friends shared things that they asked from the shell and they always remembered to say please and thank you.

Arisa Gohar (4)

Mysterious Woman In Gloves

One sunny day, while in the park playing, a weird looking woman approached me. I said hello, she did not answer.

'What are you doing?' I shouted. 'I'm playing a game here.'

The woman pulled something from her bag, I noticed her strangely large nose. She gave me the weird looking thing, I don't know why because I didn't even know her.

Suddenly the sky turned grey and she laughed an evil laugh. I tried to run away but somebody was grabbing my leg from underneath the grass. It was a woman, wearing gloves, just like the one in front of me. It was weird; there were many women around wearing gloves.

I stepped on the hand but it did not let go. I fell to the ground and used my other leg to kick the hand off. I became more terrified.

Finally my leg was free, but the broken hand was still attached. I got up and started running and screaming for dear mercy.

Suddenly the sky turned blue again, I stopped and turned round, the woman and everyone wearing gloves had disappeared. I lived in peace for the rest of my life.

Dalvane Andrew (8)

Lost In The Desert

I am lost in the desert. It's not my fault. We were having a tour of the Sahara Desert - we were allowed to get off the coach for a bit, I fell asleep and they left me there.

When I woke up I couldn't find any tracks the coach might have left so I just sat in the shade of a cactus. I began to get really thirsty; I tried to ignore it. I knew that cacti held water but if I cut it open there wouldn't be any shade for me.

Suddenly I saw a figure in the distance; someone had come to rescue me! I jumped for joy. After a few minutes I saw that it wasn't human company as I had expected, it was a camel!

The camel walked right up to me, dropped down and gave me look that said, *get on my back and I'll take you home*. So I got on his back and he walked off without a care in the world.

As he walked I told him about Mum and Dad and how we came to Africa for our summer holiday. He did take me home and he became my friend.

Isabella Colletta (11)

A Summertime Mystery

Scarlet and Harmony Smith were twins, with dark brown hair and ocean blue eyes. When the girls were eight years old, they moved house. Well, their house wasn't really a house; it was the coolest car anyone had ever seen! It had a room full of all different foods, from all over the world, a cinema suite, (including a smoothie bar), twelve legs that moved at one hundred miles per hour, wings that made it soar in the sky like an eagle, a balcony and four comfortable beds. Are you wondering how much this car cost? £50,000! It was called Turbo Wings and was the longest car in the world.

On the summer evening of their sixteenth birthday, Turbo Wings suddenly transformed into a gorgeous ship! They dived off the boat and swam to a rock pool with shimmering turquoise light from the moon.

Suddenly Scarlet and Harmony began to shiver. Their legs were unstoppable and dragged the girls under the water! Scarlet and Harmony thought they were going to drown, but they found themselves breathing. Breathing underwater? That is just silly, but it wasn't. Do you know why? Because they had transformed into beautiful mermaids.

Georgia Percival (9)

Enigma

As I walked up the narrow, rocky mountain path, my whole body shook with terror. I was nearing the top. I gulped and carefully picked my way through the endless piles of rock and human bones. Finally I rounded the corner, exhausted from the steep incline. I wrung my hands and called out nervously,

'Oh, mighty Enigma, I wish to pass through, tell me your riddle.'

The summer sun beat down on my back and sweat poured down my forehead. Then a slender figure slunk out of the mouth of the cave. The coat of her muscly, lioness body shimmered in the sunlight.

She sat, cocked her head, (resembling that of Aphrodite), to one side and sang, 'What has four legs in the morning, two at noon and three at night?'

My mind went blank, I then remembered an old song that my mother used to sing, referring to life as morning, midday and evening.

I suddenly blurted out, 'A human! A baby crawls on four legs, an adult walks on two, the elderly use a walking stick.' I was correct, I could tell. The Enigma shook all over before bursting into flames, screaming. Then she was gone …

Sara Ashleigh Graham (10)

Chimera

The bright summer sun hit me as I faced the Chimera. All around plants were green and vibrant, displaying all the summertime glory. Beads of sweat rolled off my face. The massive lion's head pulled its lips back over its teeth and let out a ferocious snarl. Simultaneously, the slender body and head of a snake where the tail should have been, hissed.

The creature flexed its mighty claws and the head and neck of a goat bleated. The lion roared a trail of flames, which I barely managed to dodge. It reared and leapt at me. I rolled out of the way, but one of the vicious claws caught my arm. Blood ran from a deep cut.

I stumbled to my feet, drawing my sword. It prepared to attack again, it lunged, I ducked and held my weapon high, driving it deep into the creature. But, as it fell, the snake head threw itself at me and plunged its venomous fangs deep into my leg. I raise my sword and cut the serpent, lion and goat's heads off, before sinking to the ground.

I had done it, but was I done too?

Voices called from far away …

Daniel James Graham (8)

Summer Story

It was a hot summer's day, I was on the Yorkshire moors, it was just me and my parents. I saw the ruins of an ancient wall, something was glowing. I felt something smooth so I picked it up. With a flash of light I was in a castle hallway, out of nowhere came a man's voice, 'You're late, the Queen is waiting.'

I followed the man, he led me to a huge room. A Tudor feast had been prepared, I was placed next to Queen Elizabeth! I was hungry so without a thought I stuffed my face.

Hours went by, we talked about the war between England and Spain, everybody thought I was the daughter of the Duke of York.

I heard footsteps, a voice said, 'Can't wait to meet the Queen.' It was the real daughter!

With a flash of light, I was on the moors again, I had been very lucky. I wondered what would have happened if I hadn't come back.

The ruins had vanished, Mum was calling me. I was amazed, only a minute had passed. My parents surprised me with a picnic, it had all my favourite things.

'Sorry Mum,' I said, 'I'm not very hungry.'

Bethany Wilson (10)

Dad, Tiddles And The Old Oak Tree

When our neighbour, old Mrs Singer, went on holiday, we looked after her mischievous ginger cat, Tiddles, for her.

On the third day, after a satisfying lunch of sardines, Tiddles decided to climb the enormous oak in our garden. He was stuck at the top for half and hour until Mum saw him, fur on end, clinging on for dear life. Dad tried to call the fire brigade, but Mum hid the phone. So Dad propped the ladder up against the tree while we held it.

At first he tried bribery, 'Puss, who's a good Tiddles? Tuna? Yummy tuna!' That didn't work. So, gingerly Dad climbed amongst the branches. As he reached out to grab Tiddles the cat clawed at him and jumped down.

Everyone cheered.

'Richard, come down,' yelled Mum.

'I can't,' he whimpered.

We tried bribing, 'Who's a good Dad? Cake? Chocolate cake!' Surprisingly enough it didn't work.

Eventually we called the fire brigade, who laughed like crazy and drank gallons of tea.

When Mrs Singer came for Tiddles, she asked if he'd been good.

'Perfect,' Dad replied, 'like a little angel.'

Ava Murtagh (10)

The Baby Goat

It was a summer holiday, the whole family was travelling to Nigeria. We stayed in Lagos for two weeks with our cousins.

On a Saturday we went to the beach. We played with the magnificent golden sand and had KFC, which was so delicious.

After a few more days, we went to the market, movies and a shopping centre called Shoprite. When we arrived at our cousin's house I was so exhausted that I had an early night.

The next morning, before I knew it, it was time to go to Ilesha, my daddy's town. The lot of us left our cousin's house in a hurry. Three hours later we arrived at Ilesha. I was so surprised because I saw so many animals on a free range, gathered together in a crowd. I moved closer to see the animals, only to spot a baby goat with a sprained leg. I felt sorry for the goat so I bandaged the leg, then my mum called me to have some milk.

When I finished the milk I remembered the goat was crying, I looked for my old feeding bottle and gave the goat milk. A few minutes later the goat jumped up, he seemed well. Then the owner came and thanked me, she gave me some Coke.

The goat thanked me by saying baaa. Then I said baaa back to him and went back to my home.

Maria Olagunju (9)

The Magical Adventure

Once upon a time, there was a beautiful princess who lived in Greece. She lived in a beautiful palace made from crystal and glass.

Each morning when the sun shone on the palace it sparkled and shimmered like diamonds. Everyone called her the Sparkling Princess.

One morning, as she was having her breakfast on a silver platter, she thought what a lovely day for the beach. As she strolled along the gentle waves lapped around her feet. It was lovely and cool in the water.

Suddenly a little voice called out to her, 'Hello, my name is Seraphina and I live in the sea, would you like to come and swim with me?

The Sparkling Princess took the mermaid's hand and they swam together. They swam together under the sea to the Kingdom of Mermaids. The princess had tea and cakes with all the mermaids and soon they were all best friends.

'Can I come again?'

'Yes,' said the mermaid as she took the princess back to the shore.

From then on the Sparkling Princess went to the beach every morning hoping she would see her new friend again, but she never returned to the shore. The Sparkling Princess never forgot her mermaid adventure.

Sophia Lowe (12)

Falling

Bang! all of a sudden smoke and flames rose from one of the plane's engines. Down, down, down we fell, the speed at which we fell was unbelievable. I couldn't hear anything as the sound was deafening. I couldn't feel much apart from the wind against my face. Breathing was hard and I lunged to grab for something, anything, something to stop me from crashing into the debris, which was following me to Earth.

This was a major moment as then the plane turned on its side and a window burst through. My ears popped as sounds came back to me. Now smoke was beginning to fill the plane, so I grabbed my nose and leapt through the window as this seemed my only option. I couldn't believe, all I could see was sea ...

Then maybe it was my lucky day after all ...

It all went black ...

Oliver Morwell Neave (10)

Charlie's Big Summer Machine

One hot day, Charlie woke up with a smile on his face because it was the summer holidays. Charlie started getting dressed when an idea popped out of his head. It was making a big summer machine.

Charlie started to make it outside. He started off by making the bottom part first, then the medium part second and after that the roof and finally the door.

When it was finished Charlie went inside the summer machine and drove off to all of his friends' houses so they could come on the summer machine to have a party.

First Charlie went to get his best friend, Michael, then Stuart and after Dan and finally Jake. When they were all on the big summer machine Charlie said that all of his friends and himself were going to have a party inside the summer machine.

Charlie gave some cakes to everybody and some drinks as well, until Dan and Jake spilled their drink on the floor, so then Charlie had to get a cloth to wipe it up. Then Michael's cake went into his nose and came out of his mouth. Eeeeeew!

After that the party was spoiled so everyone went back home.

Hugo Trent Boland (8)

The Treasure Box

Once upon a time, in a faraway land, there was a girl called Alice. She had long, golden hair with clear blue eyes, a cute button nose and a sweet shimmering smile.

One day she was walking in the woods when she came upon a treasure map. She grabbed her bag and went looking for the treasure.

Alice went over hills and mountains in search of the treasure.

After a day and a half she suddenly saw a pirate in the distance, he was wearing neon orange clothing. Alice hid behind a barrel, which creaked in the wind. The pirate stumbled past, smelling of smoke. Alice crept away and then ran straight into two pink-spotted trolls who were guarding the tunnel.

While they were fighting Alice slipped through. She clambered over the branches and came upon the shipwreck. Alice was exploring the shipwreck and in a dark corner found a dusty box. She flicked the catch and it sprang open and inside - money!

Emily-Jane Bayliss (11)

A Present For Granny

Poppy and Max's granny was poorly, so they decided to go out and buy her a present. As they walked through the woods they came across a castle with a big, dusty, red door.

They opened the creaky door and went inside the castle, where they saw a humungous table.

Poppy and Max decided to crawl under the table, but it was dark. They were so surprised to see a trapdoor in the shadows. Max opened the door and saw steep, dusty stairs full of cobwebs. They went down the stairs and a speck of light hurt their eyes.

There were two tap-dancing dragons, one green with pink spots on it and one was purple with blue spikes going up his neck.

Then a huge flame came out of the dragons' mouths and they disappeared. On the floor lay a flame coloured jewel. Max excitedly picked up the jewel and they ran back as quick as they could and gave it to Granny, she loved it!

But Poppy and Max never did tell their granny where they got the jewel from, it was their big secret!

Where will their next adventure be?

Ella Sawford (7)

Pirates Of The Dead

Once upon a time, there was an adventurer called Lennie. He had a dog called Biter. Biter was a fearless dog.

One day they found a graveyard in the middle of an island surrounded by the Atlantic Sea. The island looked haunted and they noticed a shipwreck in the ice. They decided to go inside the ship and found treasure!

The treasure had a giant golden bell on the top. They rang the bell and this woke up the dead! They heard all the pirates on the old ship shouting, 'Who dared ring the bell?'

The adventurer, Lennie, was looking into the eye of the captain of the old ship, Lennie said, 'Who are you?'

The captain answered with a hearty laugh, 'I am Blackbeard and I dare you to fight me and my crew!'

Lennie took out his whip and the fight began.

While Lennie was fighting, Biter was stealing the treasure. Biter heard a bang from the top deck and ran to see what was what. He found Lennie lying dead! Biter barked at Blackbeard and then Blackbeard took out his sword and killed him too!

Their fans never saw Lennie or Biter again, their bodies were never found, only Blackbeard knows the full story and he continues to defend his treasure.

Mitchell Dawson (7)

Where Cats Come From

It gazed down upon its darkened kingdom with glowing, golden eyes, pointed teeth and sharpened claws, capable of ripping flesh from bone. Its ears were pointed, like the Devil's horns and it had wiry black fur. Its tail twitched as it crouched down and pounced on a small creature …

Coral sat, awake, in her bed and watched as her black kitten snored gently. Occasionally his hind leg would twitch and Coral would stroke his gleaming fur to calm him. Coral remembered a friend of hers who had hated cats because she believed they were unlucky and could see ghosts. Of course Coral didn't believe it, why should she?

Suddenly, her kitten awoke, its green eyes wide with fear and it pupils adjusting to the light. His ears swivelled towards the doorway, where a dark figure began to emerge. The kitten turned to Coral and miaowed once; it could have been a goodbye or an apology, even a cry for help …

'I have come!' declared the figure in a booming voice, 'to take all cats back to where they came from and all must go again …'

Juliet Turner (12)

The Unknown Land

The computer crashed; lights went out and the signals were lost. We were flying at 5,000 feet, up above the Arctic Sea and the passengers were beginning to panic.

I could see a thunderstorm ahead and there was also a snowstorm. There was no time to stop - we had to go through it.

Suddenly I saw the Christmas lights twinkling down below through the mist and I made my decision that I was going to land in an unknown land.

I pointed my nose down towards the icebergs, reduced my speed and, as I landed, I could see polar bears and reindeer running across the ice. Slowly I came to a halt; a sleigh drawn by reindeer, with a big man dressed in a red costume flew past me. Who was this? Where was I?

Ten years later, we were still living in the unknown land in harmony. My passengers had built a little village of igloos and we had fun everyday playing polar bear tig and fishing.

What a wonderful dream for an aeroplane to live in the unknown land - the Christmas land!

Howard Weyman (11)

Another World

In Moonacre Woods I was being chased by several black, hairy dogs. I sprinted into a gloomy cave. I was truly terrified.

I ran and ran, but suddenly I fell down a hole, hidden by leaves and everything went black.

When I woke up I felt sick and dizzy, I slowly realised that I was in a small, dark room. In the corner there was a table with a note on it saying, ‘Go left and it’s the end of your track, go right and don’t look back.’

I approached the left track and I could smell the boiling lava from within. I backed away and took the right track. On the ceiling there were bats with golden eyes. I ducked as two bats flew past my head, so I ran into another room. There was a small chink of light on a box with jewels on it.

Just then I felt the hairs on the back of my neck stick up, as I turned around I saw a green troll. I screamed as loud as I could, but no one heard me. The troll very kindly opened the box, then a flash of light appeared and I was in another world …

Anna Coughlan (9)

Nessi

Once upon a time, there lived a monster in River Kess. His name was Nessi the Biter. He ate anything, but usually preferred humans.

Some humans were so scared of Nessi the Biter they didn't even look at River Kess. The fishermen were in danger.

Sam was an old fisherman, he had a son called Tom. Tom was really brave, he always tried to save people and said he would save his dad one day. They usually ate three fishes, which they had to share.

One day Sam the fisherman was going fishing in River Kess. It was calm and sunny. Sam started fishing. A minute was just about over when something heavy and long tried to force him right into the middle of the river. It was Nessi! Sam threw his fishing rod at Nessi, but Nessi just ate it. Sam tried to run, but it was too late. All the other fishermen ran away. Tom came running and threw his fishing rod's hook right at Nessi's face, it made a cut.

Nessi was dead and Sam and Tom lived happily ever after.

Muhammad Ibrahim Beg (8)

Vampires Show Themselves

One night, centuries ago, inside an old tavern called the Edengot Inn, were two drunk men, trying to make a lord laugh. Their names were Sid, Mike and Rupert, the lord.

Sid was the first man to speak, ‘So a vampire said to her son, you missed dinner - we had guests, they were delicious!’

‘That’s rubbish!’ said Mike.

‘Well, it’s not as if you could do better,’ retorted Sid.

‘Listen,’ cut in the lord, sounding rather bored, ‘as much as I would love to listen to you two squabble, I need to ask the landlord a question.’

So leaving Sid and Mike fighting like children, off went Rupert.

‘Tell me landlord,’ enquired Rupert, ‘where do you get this fine blood?’

‘Sir, that’s lager and lime,’ whispered the landlord.

‘Oh, well, thank you … I will just be leaving then, aaaahhhh!’ screamed Rupert whilst fleeing.

‘Nothing to see here, go back to your drinks,’ ordered the landlord.

Rupert and twelve other vampires sat at a round table, they called themselves Bites of the Round Table. They discussed their problem and luckily it was decided that they would live with the humans, instead of consuming them and they did.

Jonathan Evans (10)

The School Talent Show

'Hi, my name is Georgia.'

The school talent show was coming soon and I signed up. The only thing was I didn't know what to do. Lots of kids at my school were doing lots of stuff, like singing, dancing, telling jokes or magic tricks. See, whenever I get on the stage I'm like a bag of nerves. There wasn't much point, because one of my friends won two years running.

My friend won the talent show and I'm happy for her.

Georgia Hirshall (10)

The Longest Summer

One beautiful day a boy went to Ireland. His name was Oliver Todd. It was the summer holiday and Oliver is always happy when it's the holidays because he likes to rest his hand from all that writing!

On the first day out they won a fantastic game. It was called Total Action Football. As soon as he got home he played on it.

'This is the bestest game ever!' said Oliver.

Then Dad came upstairs, 'What's all the shouting for?' he said. Oliver shrugged his shoulders and Dad then went downstairs. Oliver then went to bed and happily fell asleep.

The next day, a boy called Joshua knocked on the door and asked Oliver's dad, 'Is Oliver allowed to play on the street?'

'Yeah, I'll go and get him,' said Dad. Oliver went out and that day was also good.

When Oliver had to go back to his school in England, he didn't go because he wanted a new life in Ireland.

Joshua Staniland (8)

Dennis, The Hero

When my dad lost his job we had to live on a boat. We went to travel the world. My mum wasn't very happy about it, so she told me that she was going to fake being ill so we could go back home.

We took turns to steer the boat, we brought my mum and dad and the dog. When it was my turn to steer the boat, I lost control and my dog fell overboard. I went to go and get him but the boat sailed away. I panicked, when I started to sink, my dog pulled me up from the water and paddled to the beach. It looked very deserted.

I was waiting on Lost Man's hill, but I could not see anybody coming. I saw something sticking out of the sand, my dog and I started to dig. We could not believe our eyes, we found buried treasure.

We wrote *Help* out of pebbles on the beach and started a fire. Dennis Taylor flew over in his helicopter and he rescued us.

He took us back home and I was so happy to see my family again, the treasure made us rich.

Erin Nicklin (7)

Treasure Island

It was a dark and stormy night and Blackbeard's pirate crew had set sail, in search of the unknown treasure.

Legend said whoever found it would have unlimited riches forever.

'Get your backs into it lads, if we want to find that treasure you need to work harder!' Blackbeard would bellow. They would all murmur, 'Yes,' like robots.

They travelled for 40 days until they eventually reached a large island in the middle of the sea. It had a single palm tree and the rest was sand, at least that's what they thought. What they didn't know was that there was a secret passage in the tree. They found it in the end though.

Then, soon after, Blackbeard fell into quicksand, his crew hated him, so they left him there.

They did find the treasure, there was all sorts; golden rings, rubies and much more. They had unlimited riches, but what happened to Blackbeard?

Well that will be told another day …

Aisling Bevan (11)

The Mysterious World

A light glowed under my bed. I crawled through the gap. There was a bright flash.

I glanced around. Where was I? Strange creatures were everywhere, with the heads of sharks and the bodies of lions! Their wings were covered in fluff. I thought my eyes were deceiving me. I blinked hard to make the monsters disappear, but it didn't work. I screamed.

'Stop screaming, it's deafening me,' said the creature, 'I'm a Shion. I suppose you've never seen one before?'

I stared at the Shion. 'I guess not,' muttered the Shion. I was frozen like a statue on the spot. Was this a dream?

'What are you?' questioned the Shion.

I shook my head, 'This is a dream,' I whispered to myself, 'so I shouldn't be scared.' I cleared my throat, 'I'm a human being. Not as disgusting as you!'

The creature roared loudly. In a startling flash all the Shions formed a circle round me! I gulped. One of them pounced and scratched me! I cried.

Suddenly there was a flash, I was in my bed. I glanced at my arm, it was bleeding! I couldn't believe it, it hadn't been a dream!

Nika Majidi (11)

A Summer To Remember

Yes! It's summer, no more homework, no more getting up early. I can do whatever I want, like stay out with my friends all day and stay in bed as long as I want, well until my mum pulls off the covers, saying, 'You're not staying in bed all day.'

I was out with my two best mates, Sammy and Jordan. We were playing our favourite game, truth or dare. Bad mistake! As we were walking past the most haunted house in our village, 'I dare you Freddie, to knock on the door and go in,' Jordan said. I gulped, my stomach felt like it was coming out of my mouth. As my hand reached the knocker, the door creaked open.
I popped my head in to see what was there.

I walked along the squeaking floorboards, trying to be quiet, my eyes were bulging up and my mouth was dry. I couldn't swallow. I held my breath, as I turned round the corner, but there was only a granny, in her chair, watching 'EastEnders'.

'Are you the paperboy, little lad?' and she offered me tea and biscuits.

Rosie Beard (12)

The Search For The Black Ripple

The sky was pitch-black and filled with grey rainclouds, not a single star was in the sky on Kariaki Island. The Ripple tribe crowded around the flickering fire, arguing over the fate of their suffering island.

'We need Akoni, he is the only one who can save us!' announced Ikaika angrily. His short, black hair blew gently in the wind. His deep, brown eyes shimmered in the light of the blazing fire, he was not happy.

'The gods will not allow this and you know that!' shouted Kaimi harshly. Ikaika lifted his head, he gave Kaimi a cold look.

'I do not care about what they think, he will help us and there is nothing you can do,' bellowed Ikaika. The discussion had ended, everyone returned to their huts to sleep.

Akoni Ripple was a boy who was raised in a foster home in Manhattan, but he was known as Andy Ripple. Sadly Andy never knew who his parents were. It was a mystery to everyone.

It was now morning in Manhattan. Today Andy was 16, he had already moved out of his old care home and into his new flat. He decided to visit his first foster home, with his two best friends, Katherine and Peter.

'I wonder what the care home is like now?' mentioned Katherine, as her two friends jumped off the bus.

'It's probably still a dump,' grumbled Peter.

They arrived outside the gates of the foster home, but something wasn't right. It looked like the home had been closed for 100 years, the paint was peeling off the walls. Also all the windows were boarded with planks of chipped wood.

'Are you sure this is the right address?' inquired Andy. The door of the home was wide open. Andy and his friends entered the abandoned home quietly. The house was silent but a strange rustling sound came from what used to be the office.

'It sounds like there's someone or something in the office, come on let's check it out,' whispered Andy.

They all crept towards the decrepit door and stepped into the room. There, in front of the them, stood a hideous creature, the creature's skin was grey and cracked, the cracks were full of boiling lava.

'Hello Andy, I've been expecting you,' growled the creature.

'Mrs B, is that you?' asked Andy quietly, the creature sounded like the sweet woman who used to look after him. It turned around and snarled at them, showing its sharp, green teeth.

All of a sudden it flew at Andy, he ran into the kitchen with his friends behind him. He shut the door. Suddenly a powerful feeling came over Andy, he was ready for action …

Remi Torrens (10)

The Cuckoo Clock

One day, my mum sent me to the clock shop to pick up a package. So off I went to the shop, all the way from Gamblesby to Alston.

Of course it wasn't a very good idea, because I could get kidnapped or something, but I knew I couldn't argue with my mum.

When I got there, there was a very unusual looking cuckoo clock that had got the three words - Made in Switzerland - on.

Soon enough I found myself in the Swiss Alps and there were all different coloured mountains gleaming in my eyes. But suddenly, I saw a boy, running after a bunch of goats, trying to be heard. I was just about to help the boy when I suddenly got sucked out to the clock shop.

I thought to myself, that was a very strange experience!

I walked home and gave my mum the package. And that's where my version of the cuckoo clock comes to an end.

Emily Holmes (8)

Holiday From Hell

Everything was going perfectly. I was lying blissfully under the blazing sun, my baking hot body was positioned lazily on top of a comfortable towel. My toes were stretched over and I could feel the warm sand tickling my toes.

In the distance, children were squealing in delight, as the tropical sea knocked against their legs, whilst they were attempting to jump over the waves.

The slight breeze was circling throughout the palm trees and all around men and women alike were absorbing as much of the glorious sun as possible.

We were all in the picturesque Sunny Island. People would die to go to Sunny Island and I couldn't believe my luck when I received an anonymous letter saying I'd won a holiday there.

Stupid as I was, I accepted, but now I regret it because it was all a set up and I am still on Sunny Island seven weeks later writing this to you. Waiting in anticipation for when I receive my verdict in a trial for smuggling …

Ellie Stanborough (12)

The Magic Caterpillar

One fine summer's day, a lovely little boy called Luke was out playing in the garden. Suddenly, he spotted a blue thing shining brightly. As he got closer to it, it started to take shape as a caterpillar. As soon as Luke saw it was a caterpillar he grabbed it and took it inside. When he found Mum, in the kitchen, as usual, he put it right next to her. Now, you should have seen Mum's face when she saw the caterpillar, she totally freaked out.

Just then, Luke noticed that the caterpillar's mouth was bursting with horrible blue goo! One of the bits of goo landed on the boiling hot kettle. The next thing Luke and his mother knew was that the kitchen was covered in hot water. Next the caterpillar approached the toaster.

'Not the toaster!' squealed Mum and the caterpillar looked at her as if to say, 'Yes, the toaster.'

Sooner or later Mum had dialled 999 and phoned the fire brigade. Meanwhile, Mum covered the caterpillar with a bowl.

The fire brigade arrived, 'Where's the fire?' shouted one of them in a very low voice. Soon enough they lifted up the bowl and saw the caterpillar.

'Hooray!' shrieked the whole fire brigade together. 'We've been looking for this everywhere,' said a fireman.

It turned out that Doctor Bug had been experimenting with caterpillars. Unfortunately, one had got away! The firemen were so relieved having found it again, and so happy that they gave Luke a prize, it was a fantastic robot toy.

Leah Housego-Bridgeman (8)

If I Could Be An Eagle

If I could be an eagle I'd travel the world, see different places, maybe go to a different world, I'll have to wait and see.

I would try and touch the sky, maybe that would be a challenge. I'll have to wait and see.

If I could be an eagle I'd fly in joy, I would not stop until I could reach the top, I'll have to wait and see.

Now that I'm an eagle I shall do all of those amazing challenges.

Let me reach the sky.

Ewan Smith (11)

Dorset To Desert

I sat on Poole beach. I was alone with Dad whilst the others went for a paddle. So I picked up my favourite bucket and told Dad I was going for a shell hunt. He agreed to come.

Soon we stumbled across a hole, with steps leading down. I followed the sandy steps down, they seemed to go on forever.

All of a sudden I heard voices. A few steps further on the steps came to an end. In front of me were men in Victorian clothes, knocking a hole in the wall. Amongst the rubble I saw a book. I bent down to pick it up, the cover read 'My Diary, Howard Carter 1922'.

I then realised I was amongst the Tutankhamun expedition. I looked around, there were a lot of Egyptian paintings on the walls.

At that moment the men broke through and light shone through to the antechamber. One man peered through, I overhead him say that there were loads of gold artefacts.

He said, 'We cannot go any further Howard.'

'Why?'

'They say he who enters this burial chamber will be cursed.'

I picked up the diary and scarpered. 'Dad!'

'Where have you been, Chanel?'

Chanel Marbrow-Wright (11)

Summer Land

Alex lived in Australia. He always seemed happy but he wasn't because he missed his cousin, James, in England.

One day, while digging on Manly Beach he saw a trapdoor. He went through to find himself in front of a neon sign saying *Summerland*. He kept going. There were lollipop trees and it was very hot.

Suddenly he saw an alien, he went up to it and asked it how to get to James.

It said, 'You go straight on and take the first left and then you will arrive at a pipe, go through it and you will be in his bedroom. One more thing, Evil Alien Al has set traps in some pipes.' Alex thanked him then set off. When he got there he went into the tunnel.

Suddenly he fell over a trip wire! He heard a rumbling and saw a burning ball rolling towards him. he ran as fast as he could, but it was gaining on him. Then he saw a trapdoor in the ceiling, he jumped, grabbed the handle, dodged the rolling ball and swung himself into James' bedroom.

James and Alex played happily for the rest of the day.

James Odwell (10)

Back At School Already

Where am I? thought Vicky. *Ew, there's something on my leg*. This thought sent shivers down her spine, in front of her was a large, black castle that matched the sky.

'I thought it was summer.' So like every child would, she cried. She was only 6. It was so tempting to walk inside, so, because she loved adventure, she did.

But the minute she opened the door, 'Argh!' She fell right through a black hole! Down there was a … a staff room? Wait, it was all coming back to her, it was just like the staff room at school.

Summer was over, she was back at school!

Wait, hold the relief, why was it in a large, black castle? Her school was big, but bright orange bricks, the whole building stood very proud, this one humped over.

Was she really back at school …?

Isabella Singer (9)

Sweet Dreams

I woke up one morning, the sun was shining. I knew it was going to be a fabulous day. I felt a bit strange as if I was still asleep but I could hear my mum shouting at me so I slowly walked down the stairs. Everything had changed, my house had turned into a tropical island!

My mum was standing at the bottom of the stairs wearing a Hawaiian outfit.

She said, 'No I am not mad, but you know how I said we couldn't go on holiday? I thought I'd bring the holiday to us.' My mum had set up a treasure hunt for me, so I made my way round the island looking for the flags, it was like a mini adventure.

The views from the top of the mountains were fab. I was having great fun, I had finally finished, I had found all ten flags! I had seen so many things on my adventure.

I went up to my room that night and dreamt of my own adventure.

Jessica Gilmour (12)

Once Upon A Time

Once upon a time, Elouise and Keenan went on a treasure hunt, it was exciting. They decided to go to the seaside to find treasure. Elouise found a hole, Keenan thought the treasure was in there. They dug it out more. It was fun trying to find the treasure.

There was no treasure in the hole, so they went by the sea to find some holes. They checked all of the holes that they could find.

Keenan said, 'Yes! Elouise, we have found the treasure!'

'Yay!' We finally found the treasure,' said Elouise.

Keenan and Elouise took the treasure to school to show the class. Everyone loved it in the class, even Miss Parkin too.

Elouise Gough (6)

Mystery Island

Centuries ago, by the coast of Cornwall, there was a small village called Treherne, where two fisherman named Bobby and Aidan lived.

Every morning Bobby and Aiden would go fishing and return in the evening with a feeling of success.

One morning, as they were leaving on their boat, a mysterious man appeared, only to say,

'Perhaps ye fishermen would be interested in the legendary Finland fish. It's said every fish imaginable will be there, ye interested?' he asked before disappearing without a trace.

Bobby and Aiden stared at each other before racing into the sea to find this Finland.

As fog surrounded the boat they couldn't see and soon enough they were lost in the ocean. Hours passed, when suddenly there was the chirping of seagulls above. That meant one thing … land ahoy!

As they secured the boat they were surprised to see it was inhabited. The people had red, spiky hair and light brown skin, which was covered with suspicious lilac symbols. They also wore long, straw skirts and brown, leather sandals.

'Welcome,' a man said, as the people showed them over the island. There was a tall waterfall and boats, it was Utopia.

How could life be better?

Julia Kirsty Shufflebotham (11)

Cordy's Day Out To The Beach

One morning, I went to the beach with my mum and my puppy called Cordy. It was her first time out. I cuddled Cordy all the way to the beach and I told her all about the fun she would have.

When Cordy got out of the car she was very excited. We took her onto the sand and she started digging a hole, it was so funny as she tried to bury her head. She walked to the sea and leapt back as it splashed her paws and she ran forward and barked at it.

We had lots of fun all day and when it was time to go, Cordy fell asleep with me all the way home.

Leoni-Beth Claire Burns (9)

Murder Mystery

It was a beautiful summer's day, the CSI team (Craig, Wills, Drake Walker and Nick Black), were finding their new investigation. They did eventually find it the following day, on the Sunday evening around 6 o'clock.

All of the team went to the desert to find a body where the scene of the crime happened. A young boy, aged about seven, went missing when he was on a safari tour in Egypt, none of the crew knew whether he was alive or dead.

'We have to find this boy, he is the third boy to go missing this week!' Craig shouted on the way to the desert.

'You do notice something, there's a sort of pattern, you say that three boys have gone missing this week, well, think about it, they have all been seven years old. Alex Bride, seven years old, from Edinburgh, went missing when he was walking to the shops with his aunty. Mark Livingstone, seven years old, from California, went missing when he was on holiday in Turkey, now we have Nathan King, brother of Samantha King, missing when he was on a safari tour in Egypt,' added Nick.

The three boys arrived at the crime scene just in time to see that the police were already there and found out that they had found the three other boys and they were not dead, but still alive, but badly injured.

'Well, where did you find them?' Drake didn't hesitate to ask the police.

'We found the three boys kidnapped, in the back of a man and woman's van. The man was in his early fifties and the woman in her late forties. Both of them now arrested,' Sergeant Smith told the CSI team.

Amy Johnston (11)

The Sea Has Secrets

It was an ordinary summer's day and 9-year-old Zia was enjoying swimming in the balmy sea, while her mother read a book on the beach. Zia swam a bit too far and suddenly she kept going underwater. She started swimming in desperation but her struggling was pointless and she lost her voice. She gasped for air in vain, then everything faded into darkness.

Zia woke up and found herself lying on the seabed, but somehow she was breathing and there were mermaids all around her.

She wanted to stand on her feet, but soon realised that they had turned into a shiny, scaly tail.

The mermaids told Zia that she had drowned and turning her into a mermaid was the only way to save her life. She swam up to the surface and called her mother who was searching for her with other people. But nobody could see or hear Zia.

Since then, Zia lives in the sea, but she swims to the shore every day to see her mother, who also comes to the beach every day, but her mother can't see her.

They live in two different worlds now.

Shereene Arjumand Qobil (11)

Me, My Mate And Miley

I was going to a friend's house, so I needed to get the bus. When I got to the bus stop I knew I was extremely late. I missed the bus! I didn't know what to do.

Suddenly a luxurious, lilac limousine pulled up beside me. Who was it? I wondered. The tinted window rolled down.

I screamed. It was the glamorous Miley Cyrus!

'Excuse me, do you know the way to go to get to Dublin? I'm performing there.'

'Sure,' I said in total awe. I showed her the way.

'Thanks a lot,' she said. 'Is there anything I can do for you? Oh, I know,' Miley beamed, 'I'll give you two tickets to my concert, plus backstage passes.'

'Thanks,' I exclaimed. She drove off.

I called my mum and explained, she came and took my friend and I to the concert.

When we arrived we got to the front row. Lights flashed, music blared, the audience was in an uproar. Miley entered the stage, excitement took over.

Backstage, after the concert, we met the band. It was tremendous. I'll never forget that night, it was the best experience of my life.

Brónach Falls (11)

Great Holiday

I arrived in Cyprus on a very hot day. I played with my friends around the pool most days, I also went in the sea with my snorkel and saw lots of fish. I went on a boat trip on the Coca-Cola boat, it was amazing, seeing all the sights. Then we stopped for a swim in the sea, it was 20ft deep. After the swim we headed back to shore.

The best day of all was when we went to the water park, it is the biggest in Europe. It was based on Greek Gods. It had a wave machine, it was awesome. It took you up, down and sometimes under the water.

I went on most rides except Hercules, my dad went on it and even he said it was scary.

So then we headed home from a great holiday and now we're back in Leeds.

Jessica Holdsworth (11)

Abandoned Adventurer

Abandoned! That's the only way to describe it. Abandoned!

Well, I suppose it wasn't exactly the crew's fault. I was washed ashore with no one coming to find me - I thought I was abandoned. I was ten years old when it happened.

I'm an orphan, I was sailing to Australia to start afresh, to forget the car crash, to forget the screams, to forget everything. There was a storm and I wandered on deck. Shep, my dog, followed me naturally. All I remember was a blackout; cold water in my eyes, salt gushing up my nose. That's how it all started.

I found an island, laid there for a bit and then got to work. I built a tree-house, signal fire and a bed of leaves. I woke up every day, caught a rabbit, skinned it with a stick and sat by the signal fire - hoping and waiting for a ship to come and rescue me.

But I'm 18 today and I've got a problem, no ship has come for the last eight years. I don't know whether to give up hope, I think I will, I'm happy here - I'm used to it on my own. I'm an adventurer.

Megan Davis (12)

A Horseback Ride

This story starts with a young girl called Lucy.

Lucy was so happy, it was summer, until she got bored because she had nothing to do! But her doctor rides and took Lucy to a stable called Willow Trekking Centre and she rode a little pony called Rusty. Lucy loved Rusty and she loved horses and really, really wanted to ride for the rest of her life. Her doctor did not tell Lucy that she'd booked a lesson for her until the next week.

The next day Lucy went tack shopping. When she got into riding she could not stop. Horse posters were all over her bedroom wall and to think, three years later she would be working there and she'd be an experienced rider - you never would have guessed!

Lucy Perkins (10)

The Mysterious Classroom

The day passed by and it had become night in school. All the staff had left and it was pin-drop silent. Unexpectedly there were sounds coming from a year 6 class.

'Oh, great, the teacher left the tap running again,' cried one of the paintbrushes sitting by the edge of the sink. 'I'd shut off the tap but I don't have hands, you see,' he moaned.

'Oh yes, that is true, there, it's off now. Oh no, my blades have scratched the tap! Poor tap, I really do hope the teacher does not notice when she comes in the morning!' quivered the scissors.

On the other side of the classroom things were not going as planned … *ping, ping, ping!*

'No, please don't throw us into the bin, please!' pleaded the plastic frogs whom the children enjoyed playing with during wet play-ins.

Tick tock, tick tock!

'Quick the teacher is coming! Everyone back to your places.

'Oh no, how did those scratches get on the tap?' wondered the teacher.

Priya Vara (11)

Dream Horse

A wonderful horse, waiting for me, as beautiful as horses can be. As chestnut brown as a tree trunk. When she jumps she hits the stars. Her deep brown eyes, like the brownest eyes you could imagine. When I give her food she does what she should.

This horse is the only one for me. I ride her from Blackbarrow End to the other end of the road.

This horse and I can't live without each other, me and you forever.

Chloe Shannon Bush (12)

The Sunshine Egg

Michael was a horrid boy, he played pranks on teachers, was foul to anybody who blocked his way and stole people's lunch money.

It was the last day of school before Michael went to the high school. As you can imagine it was boiling hot. The sun looked like it was getting closer.

Suddenly a golden egg fell just outside the school gate, so Michael hopped over to fetch it. He snuck it under his desk.

'OK class, please get your pencils out of your desks, we'll be having a test today,' bellowed Mr Shwimmer. Halfway through the test Michael's desk opened slightly and all he could make out was two golden eyes staring at him, he slammed his desk lid closed.

'Get me up into the sky or I'll eat you alive,' squeaked a voice from in his desk. Michael rushed off to the toilet. He tried in so many ways to get the creature back into the sky, but none of his ideas worked.

After school all of Michael's friends waited for him, but just a giant golden ball rolled out of school …

Kate Phillips (11)

Ghost Maze

Mesmerised we stared at Queen Victoria's crown. Despite the sign saying: Do Not Touch, Kyra and I stroked the crown. There was a creak from the floorboards and without warning a trapdoor opened. We fell, screaming, into a pool of darkness.

Abruptly our feet touched the floor. In front of us were tall, stone walls. There was a gap in the wall which seemed our only chance to find an exit so we both nervously walked through it. We were in a maze. We walked forward anticipating danger.

After a while we discovered many dead ends. We were now deep in the maze. Turning the corner a misty figure met my eyes. It was a ghost! Quickly we turned back, unnoticed. 'I have an idea.' Kyra gave me a leg up. I sat on top of the wall and pulled Kyra up. We both jumped off and walked on. My plan worked.

After doing that several times we found the exit and stairs to safety. Climbing them I wondered, does anyone know what we just discovered, that there was an adventure to have under the Tower of London? I never knew a day trip could be so exhilarating.

Tara Clancy (11)

My Phobia

I had just missed the bus home from town, so I caught the next bus half an hour later.

When I arrived, Mum screamed, 'Why are you late? You should've called me.'

I didn't even whisper, I just rushed upstairs with tears in my eyes.

'Muuumm! What have you done to my private, peaceful room?'

'I just thought that they would make your room brighter, a few ...'

'No, please don't say that feared, dreaded and disastrous name. It is terrifying.'

'Hang on, oh, I thought you were joking when you said you were scared of goldfish, sweet-pea!'

I began sulking.

The next day I got out of bed and felt brave and fearless as I said, 'This room isn't big enough for both of us!'

An hour later I'd sold my fish: £5.00 for two tiny orange goldfish!

I think I'll sell my dog tomorrow, I thought.

Anna Sumner (10)

My Summer Adventure

In the summer holidays my mum gave me a map. It was a race to find the golden cap.

As I walked down the road, I saw Willow, the neighbour's cat, I knelt down and asked, 'Have you seen a golden cap?' He miaowed at me, so that was that!

I peered through my friend's window to see if he would give me a hand, but it was no good, he was having a nap!

As I walked down the road I saw a man, singing a rap. I looked up at his cap, but it wasn't the one on the map!

Then I went to see my dad, what was that on his lap? As I moved closer I saw it shining at me.

My dad called me, 'Come and see.' And there it was, the golden cap, just the same one as on the treasure map.

Aamina Iqbal (8)

A Twist In The Tale

Sophie and John are off school and Mum and Dad are off work. It's a hot day. We're all off to the beach. We're meeting Aunt Jackie and Toby. Yippee! Toby is my best friend. He's the same age as me but he has brown hair.

After a long drive we arrive. Mum and Dad unpack our car. I'm so impatient; I can't wait to get onto the beach. Aunt Jackie and Toby have already arrived. We lay our towels out on the sand.

John and Sophie make a magnificent sandcastle. I run straight through it and get such a telling off. Everyone's scared to go into the sea. Not me - I dive straight in. We play on the beach with a frisbee and then I almost fall asleep sunbathing. It's time for the barbecue - Toby and I love sausages.

It's getting cooler. It's time to go. Sophie falls asleep in the car so Dad carries her straight to bed. John follows behind. Mum tells me to go to bed too. So, I reluctantly go into the utility room and curl up on my bed. It's a hard life being a dog!

Rowan Petrie (10)

Beautiful Beast

Looking out of my window of the wooden hut in South Africa where I live with my mother, father and three brothers and two sisters, I saw a sudden movement in the long grass. It was like a streak of lightning flying through the grass, like a ski boat as it sails through the water. All of a sudden leaping upwards, then soaring back down.

Then I realised it was a cheetah, one of the fastest creatures, reaching from 0mph to 60mph in a minute. I was so amazed by this creature, so delicate, so agile, yet so beautiful. I stood looking at it for some time, just staring. Suddenly it pounced and ran off.

That was the last I saw of the cheetah, but he'll come back, I know he will.

Jess Stoves (10)

Through The Eyes Of A Tiger Cub

I remember the days that were peaceful, quiet and calm, the days when I still had my tiger mum. But one day the metal monsters arrived and she disappeared. I was left alone and left in fear.

Then, one day, someone found me and took me home and fed me, cuddled me, I wasn't alone. I grew up fast and grew massive claws and huge teeth that ruined doors. They put me in a scary jail box, I put up a fight. Then they shut the door and locked it up tight.

They took me to a big, green place, one stared at me face to face, opened the door and let me free, I ran as fast as my paws could carry me.

Suddenly I ran into an orange thing that knocked me to the ground, she sniffed me and licked me, it was my mother I had found. We chased each other back to the cave where we had lived, but I will never forget that loving, caring kid.

Megan Tee (13)

Shaking Up Jamaica

'Sun, sea, sand, a tropical paradise,' - that was my mom's opening remark when recalling our family holiday to Jamaica, Jamaica Land We Love, (national anthem).

Our main destination was in Jamaica's cruise capital, Ocho Rios. Smiling faces, crystal waters and reggae rhythms were three of the main attractions; but having great weather as well was clearly one of the highlights of our unique two-week family holiday!

That was until Hurricane Dean struck! The hotel shook like maracas, making the island dance. Palm trees swaying, Rasta men praying, who might save the day now? My heart raced with adrenaline, wondering if this moment would pass or if fate would ensure that this was my last!

The rain came down with a roar and a rumble … but the sun came up. Jamaica's blessing, shining down with love from above!

Finally, allowing us to bite back into the Caribbean culture and experience the island buzz again, no problem!

Alydia Scott (10)

War At Heart

There was a dreary time, long ago, when children had to leave their parents as the city became too dangerous for little children, or so they said.

One special but spoilt girl decided to run away, as she definitely didn't want to live with some stranger.

The night before she had to leave, Alice crept downstairs, took her bag, then sprinted, hoping she could find her Nanna's house as Nanna would never give young Alice away. Unlucky for her, that night was the longest air raid London had ever experienced. At this point Alice had stumbled into a ditch.

'Oww!' screamed Alice. Oh how poor little Alice was frightened to death in the cold night!

A lady, called Judy, came striding past. From the corner of her eye she noticed a little girl in great pain. Quick as a wink Judy lifted Alice into her arms. In half an hour Alice was safe and sound in the hospital.

It turns out that Alice had broken her leg when she fell into the ditch. Once she had her cast on they sent her home. How her parents were relieved to see their little darling alive.

Caitlin Fotheringham (11)

Never-Angel

What's a butterfly without its painted wings? Or a sky without its gleaming sun? It would be a fathomless existence, lingering gloomily above the Earth. The sky's friend would be lost. That's exactly how I would feel without my Never-Angel.

My Never-Angel is my guidance, a map. If I were to be plummeted into an alien world my Never-Angel would tell me where to go. It has no form or body or breath, my Never-Angel is a wise presence in my mind. Pocketed into a corner I never knew.

Everyone has a Never-Angel, but most don't know it to be true. For one terrible moment I thought I had lost mine.

A car was coming round the bend towards me, the wheels were blurs. I was not scared. My Never-Angel would save me, but I felt no presence in my mind. My Never-Angel was gone. Suddenly terrified, I escaped to the grassy bank on the other side of the lane, the car missed me.

It was days later when I realised that my Never-Angel had not abandoned me. it had proved to me that I could guide myself to safety. I smiled.

Isabel Mary Head (10)

Winning Cruise

The mail came through the letter box and Demi ripped open the envelope addressed to her.

'Mum, Dad, come down, I've won! I've won a family cruise to Spain!' she cried.

'Oh Darling, that's brilliant, when is it?' her mother inquired, sounding surprisingly enthusiastic.

'Yay! Spain! The beach, the sun, the ice cream, the …' Jack, Demi's younger brother interrupted.

'Not now Jack,' Demi said loudly. As usual she paid no attention to her younger brother. Demi was so excited, she made a calendar to cross off the days. The two weeks flew by and suddenly it was the day before the cruise.

They stepped onto the plane, the minute the plane took off Jack started, 'Are we there yet?'

'No,' replied Mum. Ten minutes passed and he repeated the question.

'Are we half-way there yet?'

'No,' replied Dad. Fifteen minutes passed and he repeated his question.

'Are we almost there yet?'

'No,' shouted Mum, Dad and Demi. Then the whole family fell asleep, one after the other. They awoke and they were in Spain.

They collected their luggage, got a cab to take them to the hotel.

'Wow!' said Demi, 'I can't wait for the activities to start tomorrow.'

Olivia Singer (11)

The Trapdoor

On a Saturday afternoon, me and my mum were in the park and I saw a big hole. Me and my mum jumped into it and went through a tunnel, and we saw that at the end of the tunnel was an extremely hot forest.

There was a trapdoor there, which was locked. My mum grabbed the key and unlocked the trapdoor, there was treasure there. We got it and went back to the park by wishing.

Sophie Zeeman (8)

Maria And The Razabuzma

Maria's family were going for a picnic in Bluebell Woods. They found a nice spot by the stream and sat down. Suddenly a beautiful, eye-catching butterfly fluttered by and Maria found herself following it.

It flew into perfect sight before transforming into a strange creature. The animal whispered, 'Hello,' in a timid voice.

Maria was astounded. 'What are you?' she stammered, not sure whether to be scared or excited.

'I am a vir - very important Razabuzma, but you can call me Ronnie. I help our queen change spring into summer and you, Maria, are to be our new queen.'

'What, me, a queen! ... Impossible!' exclaimed Maria.

Ronnie said, 'You must help summer happen.' Maria felt utter disbelief, how could she be the Summer Queen?

'Less talk, more walk, we need to get to Summer Hill before sunset,' Ronnie urged.

It felt like they had been walking forever when they reached the foot of Summer Hill.

'Hill, I bring you Maria,' bellowed Ronnie.

'Maria, walk slowly up the hill,' boomed a loud voice from somewhere.

Cautiously Maria began her ascent - plants and flowers sprang up around her feet, then the voice thundered, 'See Maria, you are the Queen of Summer.'

Amelia Perring (11)

The Curious Case Of The Murdered Priest

Sir Henry Cradock sat in his small study listening to some intriguing news on his telephone. On the receiver was Superintendent Bill Higinton.

'I know you're quite good at helping the police,' he said, 'so we wondered if you could help us find a murderer that baffled the police of five counties. A priest was murdered at St Mary's Roman Catholic Church on Harrison Road.'

'How do you know it was the same man?'

'He leaves red crosses, he always does, on a white handkerchief.'

'I'll be there.' The line clicked.

At the church, Sir Henry sat watching as men checked for fingerprints.

'If only he'd left some clue,' said Sir Henry. 'Wait, what's that powder?'

'It's some chemical, we are not sure what though, it's a trail and it goes to that wall.'

'Hey,' shouted Sir Henry excitedly, 'last week I was reading an article about this church, so if I'm right,' he said, twisting a statue of an angel on the wall, 'there is your murderer'.

Behind the wall stood the arcitect of the church.

'But why?' asked a police officer.

'Because he didn't get paid,' said Sir Henry Craddock.

James Watson (10)

Midnight

It was midnight. I was still awake, wondering why I wasn't feeling sleepy. Maybe I was scared of the dark and stormy night.

Suddenly I heard a noise, a bit like thunder. I slowly climbed out of my bed to see if it was thunder. I reached to open the curtain and saw there was no thunder, just a cool breeze.

Then I noticed something moving in the garden. I couldn't see what it was in the dark. I tried to wake my dad up, but I wasn't capable enough. So I woke my big sister up. We went downstairs to look through the window, I gasped. The thing wasn't there anymore.

My sister said, 'It must have been an illusion.' I thought it couldn't have been my illusion, so I went back to sleep again. at last I could go to sleep. I told my mum and dad about last night.

The sun had set, I didn't wake anyone up, I went downstairs myself. I saw something with wings, I went outside and saw a unicorn! I thought I'd be its friend and we were.

Navjeet Kaur (9)

My Dream Cloud

I woke up on a cloud. I had no idea how I got there. What happened? I started looking around. The cloud was as white as snow and as soft as a blanket. This cloud had shops, cars and people. They spoke white clow language because I had brought a dictionary, (they used pounds by the way). I took a look before putting it in my bag, which looked new. 'How odd, a new bag!' I sat down and fell asleep and in the morning people were gathered round me.

I think they thought I was dead, so I ran away and all of a sudden I fell over.

There I was, in a hospital bed, a nurse came in looking shocked. She said my parents were outside. I told her about my dream and she laughed and said it was normal to have funny dreams in a coma.

Coma, I thought, she said I had been in a car crash, then she lifted up a bag ... it was brand new, just like the one in my dream.

'From all of us,' she said.

Martha Jane Lee (11)

When The World Ended

One dark, stormy night, the waves on the sea were as tall as the tallest tree, as strong as the strongest man. All the fish and sea creatures underneath, were being swept away by the currents. Sea horses clinging on by their tails to the remaining strips of seaweed.

On land things were not any better. Earthquakes struck from all around the world and all of a sudden the world just … collapsed!

Ashleigh Brown (10)

My Secret Slide

One bright, sunny day, me and my sister were playing on the slide in my back garden. Suddenly a trapdoor opened and I slipped through. The slide was still carrying me under the ground. The slide finally ended and I found myself on a beach. I was about to get up when something fell on my back … it was my sister, Tiarna, she must have followed me.

Me and Tiarna found a map on the sand, it said, 'Treasure over the sea.' In the distance I could see a box. Tiarna ran up to see what was inside. In the box was a shell. Tiarna picked it up and got scared because it started talking to her.

I picked the shell back up and it started to say, 'You want treasure?'

We said, 'Yes please!'

'You will have to go across the sea,' said the shell.

Me and Tiarna went on a dolphin across the sea.

'There's the treasure,' said Tiarna.

In the treasure chest were chocolate coins to eat and bracelets and necklaces to wear. Me and Tiarna fell asleep, when we woke up we were back in the garden again. Was it a dream or was it real?

Taliyah James (9)

A Tribute To The Sun Goddess

It's midnight, the fairies come out to dance. The festival of the sun goddess commences. Round the circle of the sun the fairies dance. A night of dancing until the sun rises. When the sun rises the dancing stops and the elves appear as if by magic, to present the sun goddess with a pentacle formed from the rays of Hekate. All the fairies begin to shimmer and shine and transform into beautiful doves. Doves fly everywhere and form together to create a path leading to a shimmering porthole.

The fairy princess appears out of the trees and walks the path of doves and into the porthole, strewing gold flowers as she walks.

A brilliant light shines down on the porthole and the porthole seems to evaporate!

An anxious group of fairies and elves wait for their princess to appear again and before long the brilliant light shines again and the fairy princess walks into view.

She has changed! Now she is the sun's daughter, a sun-shaped mark on her forehead and her hair the colour of the sun's rays.

Now the fairies and the elves live by the power of the sun.

Natasha Ford (12)

Fear Fears Joy

It was a warm, sunny day and I was strolling along the cliff path when a sudden gust of wind caught me. I stumbled and fell. I was clinging to the rocks for dear life. I was terrified. My heart was pounding against my chest. I could fall off the cliff at any moment.

And then I heard a voice, it was cold and hollow. 'Ha, ha, ha,' it cackled, 'you either die up here or die down there, either way you lose!' the voice gloated, 'but I'd prefer you down there. I want every ounce of fear you've got, so …' the voice tailed off.

A massive gust of wind knocked sharp bits of slate off the cliff and they were heading straight at my hands.

'My sister Joy will hear about this,' I shouted. I didn't know why, it just sounded like the right thing to say.

'Your sister who?' said the voice.

'Joy,' I repeated. I quickly moved my hands as slate hit the cliff.

'Please, I'll let you go, but please, d-d-don't tell Joy,' the voice whimpered.

'Deal.' I said and suddenly was safe back on the path.

Eva Black (9)

Pirate Pete's Perilous Voyage

The ship was heading towards Captain Jackman's lost island. Captain Jackman went to the island to find the lost treasure, but he never came back.

After a long journey, Pirate Pete and his crew finally found the island. The sand was warm from the sun and the slow waves passed. The coconut trees moved to the rhythm of the wind.

'Come on, we have treasure to find,' Pirate Pete exclaimed. Everyone cheered.

Then they came to a waterfall, they decided to rest there after their long journey. The crew enjoyed it, however, Pirate Pete told them to keep going on.

Finally they came to a cave. They entered the cave slowly, when they reached the end they heard a voice, 'Go away from this island and never come back, or you will see the consequences!' They all ran and got lost.

Pirate Pete felt scared, but suddenly he heard the waterfall. Pirate Pete and his crew followed the sound. When they got there one of the crew heard waves and coconut trees, they followed the sound, which led them back to the ship.

Pirate Pete and his crew went home and never back to Captain Jackman's lost island.

Arthi Suthagar (11)

The Adventures Of Melody

Chapter 1 - Meet Melody

'Hi, my name is Melody, I am a baby doll with a big secret. I love adventures, so in the summer holidays when my owner, Holly, is away outside playing, I go on some marvellous adventures. Last time I went on a picnic with my best friends, aka - the stuffed toy gang. Not today! Today I am going on a trip to the beach with Barbie, Ken and Jessie, the cowgirl from Toy Story 3.

But what will happen when we get there ...?

Chapter 2 - Barbie's Disappointing Surprise

'Melody, Melody,' cried Barbie, 'I have to tell you something.'

'Anything,' said Melody.

'I can't take you to the beach,' continued Barbie.

Melody was speechless, she had been looking forward to the beach trip for weeks now.

'Shall I show you why?' asked Barbie.

Melody nodded, of course she wanted to find out the cause of the stop to the beach trip. Barbie handed Melody the menu for the beach bar they were going to eat at and also a poster for the beach.

The menu read -

'Haggis, neeps and tatties
Chicken nuggets and chips with beans on the side
Fish and chips fresh from Rocky's Plaice kitchens.
Rocky's Plaice Beach Is Now Closed Due to Toxic Flood and Poisonous Snakes.'

'Oh no,' cried Melody.

Chapter 3 - Dolls On A Mission

'OK,' Melody said, 'my plan has to work. Commence Melody's super duper chocolate cakey bakey cookies plan, ABC, 123.'

'Well,' said Ken, 'I'm glad we didn't go with the long name.'

Melody scowled, '321, go!'

Jessie ran underneath the bars to the beach with a plate of Melody's super duper chocolatey cakey bakey cookies fresh from the oven and waited. The snakes came over and ate the cookies, then Ken and Barbie dropped a net over the mean snakes and put them in a truck for the local zoo.

Meanwhile, Melody had got all the toxic water in a bottle. The beach was saved! Thanks to Melody and her friends.

The owners of Rocky's Plaice, Rocky, Mrs Fish and Mrs Chips were so happy that all of the gang got free ice cream to enjoy while having a nice day out at the beach.

Holly Fleming (10)

Just Your Average Day At The Beach

We'd been sitting on the beach all day. It was dark, everyone had left. Our fire was blazing away. Dad was lighting the barbecue.

Suddenly, my sister, Rosa said, 'Alice, what's in the water?' I looked where she was pointing. Straight ahead, a 20m long snakelike creature was slithering towards us.

'Mum, Dad, look in the water!' I shouted. They saw it too.

'Okay, grab your bags, we'll just move further along the beach, don't worry,' said Mum in a panicked tone. We picked up our bags. The monster was reaching shore as we walked away.

'It's following us!' I whispered.

'Oh God,' screamed Rosa. The snake was speeding up and was growing. Its tail was in the sea but its head and body were plummeting towards us.

'Run!' shouted Dad, so we did. My feet thwacked the ground, I'd never sprinted so fast in my life. Then it hit me.

'Dad, get out the lighting fluid from your bag, throw it over the snake and light it with a match!'

Dad did just that and we stood there watching the snake burn to death as the police and paparazzi arrived.

Ella Creamer (13)

How The Snail Got Its Shell

In the days when everyone was happy, the snail lived under greyish rocks by the fast flowing stream, shaded by towering trees. The snail's home blended into the cliffs on the beach, but the rocks got too heated up by the extreme heat and snails don't like heat.

The snail said to himself, 'It's too warm, the heat is giving me a headache.'

The snail stayed under the cliff so the snail's arch-enemy didn't see him.

There was a friendly looking Goldie Gull hovering over him.

'Excuse me Mr Gull, can you tell me where to find a damp, cool and dark home for me to live in?' asked the snail.

'How am I meant to know? OK fine, I'll try.'

Without letting the snail say another word Goldie Gull scooped up the snail into his large, golden, narrow beak. The snail screamed, then looked around.

'Hey, this is a perfect home, damp, cool, dark,' he said, then fell asleep.

The snail woke up in a horse field. The snail slimed to a sand coloured horse.

'Excuse me Miss … excuse me!' shouted the snail. 'Do you know anywhere that is cold and damp, cool and dark?' the snail asked politely. But because the snail was behind the horse the horse kicked the snail past the stars.

'Wooo!' he crashed in an empty wooden barn, he saw a small spider on a silky web. 'Excuse me, can you tell me where to find a cold, cool, damp and dark place? I've asked Goldie Gull and the horse, but they didn't help me, so please can you tell me?'

'I know somewhere but you'll have to enjoy the pleasure of my company, there are some rocks and shell over in that corner,' the spider told the snail.

'Oh, really, thank you for the help,' the snail said as he slithered to the rocks and shells and fell asleep. When he woke up only his eyes and foot popped out of the shell.

Billie Collishaw (11)

Untitled

One wet, miserable summer's day, I woke up and looked out the window. I said to myself, 'Will the forecast ever get it right? Obviously not, they'll have to get some more technology to help them.' Then I thought this would the worst summer ever, but I was wrong.

The next morning it was 30 degrees. I quickly got out of bed and skipped breakfast and it was boiling outside. I sat under a tree by the river, which was lovely and shady, then I looked at the river. There was only a trickle in it and there were lots of shrimps swimming around, trying to get into the last of the water. I was watching the life around the river for five minutes. Then I decided to climb my favourite tree. I climbed as high as I could, then I was called in for lunch.

After I'd eaten my lunch, which was pasta, Max called round. We played together with my brother Peter and all three of us played in my best tree. We played with the Lego and had a Lego battle. Max was on my side and Peter was on his own. Max and I won. Max stayed for tea. After that Max had to go.

It had been the best summer ever and all the rest of the week was lovely as well.

Christopher Quinn (8)

I Became A Pirate

Once upon a time, my friends and I went to the beach. We were having so much fun that we went to sea in a boat. Because we were so far from shore and the wind and sea were calm, I slowly went to sleep.

All of a sudden I was awake. I was on a pirate ship and I had a pegleg, a hook and a parrot on my shoulder.

Suddenly another pirate shouted, 'Our ship is under attack by some other pirates!'

I said, 'Shoot at them.'

'But we have no gunpowder,' said somebody.

Another pirate walked in and said, 'We are being boarded by a girls' pirate gang.'

I looked up and saw that their ship was sinking, they weren't attacking us after all, they just needed our help.

Ever since that day the girls' gang and us pirates became one big team and were unbeatable.

Stuart Strongman (9)

Somewhere Only I Know

As I leisurely walked out of the bright blue door of my cottage I closed my eyes to the sound of the birds reciting and the sun blazing. As I walked up the slightly steep hill I could feel the sea breeze flow past me, as I looked onwards onto the church and the golf course, all calm and at ease. I felt like I was gliding as I went along the rocky footpath. Soon I was running up the sand dunes and past that … was the sweet vision of the crystal, smooth ocean.

As I swiftly dashed down a sand dune, I couldn't help but think I was in the Caribbean, I was looking for something treasured but it wasn't there. As I gradually walked towards the sea, a familiar figure emerged, staring right at me, in front of the sea. The figure was the thing I was looking for, something I had been waiting for, for 12 months. As I ran towards the man in soldier uniform, the sheer relief of compassion ignited with love! We hugged so tightly we couldn't breathe. My love was home.

Two years later he fought to his last breath.

For my love.

Molly Wooders (14)

A Day In The Life Of Me In The Summer Holidays

In the summer holidays I had a great time with my friends and family. I am going back to the first few weeks of the holiday.

So the summer holidays were well underway, me and my mum's friends had arranged to meet up. Anyway, that morning, me being me, I woke up pretty early. Full of beans, not the type you eat, but you get what I mean. So I got up, had breakfast, played on my PlayStation, brushed my teeth, had a bath, got dressed and then we waited for my mum's friend to come and pick us up, because we were all going to the cinema to see The A Team.

My mum's friend's children were coming as well and I knew them because we all went to the same primary school and we all became good friends.

Anyway, so me and my mum were sitting there, waiting and waiting and waiting … and then we heard a car pull up, it was them.

When we arrived at the cinema we had just enough time to get snacks and drinks. The movie was brilliant, we went to McDonald's for our dinner. Then we got dropped home.

Yasmin Mohammed (12)

Real Beauty

There was a girl called Selena Edwards. She was nineteen years old. She always used to look at celebrity pictures, like Hannah Montana or Rihanna and then she used to look at herself in the mirror and say my eyes aren't nice, or she used to say my nose is too big and spotty. Her parents always used to say to her, you are beautiful and you have nice, twinkling eyes and yeah, we like you the way you are. But no matter what happened, Selena always had complaints about herself.

Then, one day, one of her friends, Emily Carmen, same age as Selena, had a terrible car accident and was left with scars and had lost one eye. When Selena saw Emily's scars, she realised that God had gifted her with a nice healthy body and with a beautiful face. She realised something else too, that beauty lies in good health.

After seeing this story, of Emily Carmen involved in the accident, Selena's mind had been changed about her looks. This changed her life and she focused on all the wonderful things that were happening in her life and realised real beauty lies within you.

Ambereen Sharif (11)

Summertime In The Garden

Dad was watching the football again! I was bored and went into the garden. The garden was a mess because the council were putting in a water main. A pile of earth spilled over the barrier where they were working and in it I saw something shining. I pulled out a tiny silver box. There was writing, too small to read, engraved on it, the first letter looked like a T, I traced the letter on the box and the world spun.

The spinning stopped, I was in my garden but the pile of earth had been replaced by the swing my brother and I used to have. A young boy, who looked familiar, had his neck caught in the ropes of the swing and was turning blue. I unwound the rope, he took a deep breath, sat down and drew a T in the mud.

Suddenly I was back by the barrier, in my hands I could clearly see the words, Time Travel, glowing on the box. As I thought about what had happened, I remembered the story my brother had told me about a mysterious stranger who saved his life before I was born and I smiled.

Madeleine Smith (10)

The Giant's Footprint

'Come on Charlie, I want to try out my new fishing rod,' shouted Ben.

'All right, I'm coming now,' replied Charlie and together they set off for the stream with their father.

As they turned a corner they saw a crowd of people gathered around the bowling green. Charlie's and Ben's father pushed through the crowd, there on the bowling green was a giant footprint.

'Wow!' exclaimed Charlie,

'Super!' shouted Ben.

'Tell your mother I have gone off to report this on the news,' said their father. (He was a news reporter). So off they went home.

Suddenly Ben fell into a fast-flowing river.

'Ben!,' cried Charlie and jumped in. Ben got swept up onto the river bank. Towering above him was a giant! He was at least ten feet tall. Ben stepped on a twig.

'Mama!' boomed the giant.

'Ben,' whispered Charlie, who had climbed out beside him. Suddenly Ben and Charlie found themselves in the giant's grip. He was about to put them in his mouth when, 'Bob, bad boy,' said his mother and Charlie and Ben were put down in their garden. They smiled, what an adventure!

Mary Gardner (11)

One Adventure

Cold, dismal day, Mum at work, friends on holiday.

Okay, what shall I say … another boring day in the summer holidays, you're thinking, oh no, shut the book, right? Well don't cos it's about to get truly interesting.

Later

A rescue call … tomorrow … staying over … Auntie and Uncle's … a week! I'm thrilled, excitement! Two hours of packing and ten hours' sleep later, I know I am ready for an enthralling adventure!

We're in the car … but we're lost. The welcoming aroma of the countryside permeates as we drive past fields of green and every few minutes I hear, 'Have we missed the turn off?'

Arriving, we decide to take a walk. We walk through field and onto a road. I run ahead. Running past my school, breathing in the fresh, damp air, until I face a door. What I see is suddenly not familiar anymore. I am lost, but my curiosity doesn't stop.

The screech of a vehicle, I turn to my aunt for some security, but she is no longer there. I open the door to find a white world. People that I've never met … They were part of my family … lost them years ago …

Eleanor Baker (11)

The Undefeated . . . Me!

As I entered the stadium, the crowd went quiet. I felt my cheeks starting to burn. Then I had my spear at the ready when the barrier was lifted - and the lion approached me.

Standing up straight looking brave, I repeated the words Julius had said to me. But as it came nearer, my bravery withered. My heart started pumping and my legs started shaking, until suddenly, with a roar it leapt up into the sky, but as I lifted my spear, the animal was no more.

The cheer from the crowd declared me victorious. Then the sound faded as another poor animal was dragged out to face the undefeated me!

Eleanor Pipe (11)

The Diary Of Captain Cryer

14th November 1983:
It was a cold night last night. We all had to huddle together for warmth, the crew and I. In the morning the wind was blowing. One of my crew, old George, had his hat blown away. Poor lad!

15th November 1983:
Terrible storm last night. Kept me up. We arrived at land this morning and have been searching for the treasure all day. Sailor Fred pretended to have seen the treasure ... He walked the plank! Ha, ha!

16th November 1983:
We found the treasure! I'll go down in history for this. 'Captain Cryer, the greatest pirate of all time!'

Sophia Boni (11)

The Ticket Of Three Wishes

It was a normal Saturday morning and I was in the mood for shopping, so I phoned my friends to see if they wanted to come with me. They said yes and we arranged to meet in Cardiff at 2pm.

When we met up, we decided what shop to go to first. I said 'Build-A-Bear', Tia said 'Claire's', Libby said 'Zara'. 'New Look,' said Christina, 'Next,' said Beth.

'Stop! We have got to decide together. To make it fair we will do one shop at a time and then everyone will be happy,' I said.

After we went to 'Build-A-Bear' and 'Claires' we decided to stop for a snack. I picked up a packet of fruity pops, hoping I had the ticket of three wishes. After I had paid for it, I realised that I had the lucky ticket! I was so happy that I jumped up and down with excitement. I could never have imagined that I could be this lucky!

My first wish would be to end poverty. My second wish would be to have food and water. My third would be that I could own a sweet shop called 'Charmayne's Candy'.

Charmayne Bishop (9)

The Robbery

I saw him. He was wearing a black and white stripy sweater. At first I thought he was going to get money from his account, but then all of a sudden I heard the alarm sound and at that moment, I saw him break through the side of the bank and run to a motorbike which was quite small.

Escaping from the police, the burglar, who was on the small motorbike, pulled back his grip and accelerated from my view. I thought he was going to get away. Then I heard an officer say, ‘Stop! Burglar!’

When the level crossing barriers came down, I thought that the robber would get run over, and I think he did because I couldn’t hear the motorbike’s engine running anymore. As the train had passed and the police had gone into the distance, I saw a figure emerge from the black and white barrier. It was the robber.

Karsten Lloyd (11)

Secrets

This was it. The hot, sunny holiday I had been looking forward to for ages. My parents had finally brought me and my sister to Spain for a week and we were about to go swimming in the crystal-blue sea. I stood by the edge, the calm waves lapping at my feet. It looked so inviting and so clean!

I took a deep breath and ran! The water splashed up over my face and body and I squealed with delight. It was warm, but not too hot. I dived underneath, letting the gentle current flow around me. As I got deeper, my parents and sister going out of sight, I could see ... a castle! Wait, it couldn't be, I mean I was underwater!

It grew nearer and nearer and it was becoming very clear. It was a castle with tiny fish swimming in and out. I swam through the stone archway, taking in the beautiful sights. It was amazing! Seaweed, crabs and even dolphins caught my eye as I swam through the rocky building.

After looking around for a bit, I swam back to the surface. I couldn't wait to come back tomorrow!

Katrina Corder (11)

My Mermaid Friend

One boiling hot day, me and my family decided to go to the beach. I've always loved the beach, the golden sand around me, the fresh air and the sparkly water smiling at me, it is just so beautiful.

When we reached this lovely paradise, I sat near the water and saw something bright and colourful, so I jumped into the water and realised it was a prestigious, multicoloured mermaid. The mermaid looked at me, frightened and I whispered, 'I will not hurt you. I just want to become friends.'

Meanwhile, the mermaid came closer and grabbed my hand. We swam in-between rocks and past lots of weird fish. At the corner of a sunken boat there appeared a colony of mermaids living in an underwater castle.

My mouth was open wide and I was fascinated by the mermaids and the golden castle. Then, just a few seconds later, I realised I was a mermaid myself just because of my new mermaid friend.

Zuzanna Lechman (9)

Summer Days And Summer Nights

A perfect summer day is when the sun is shining above the sky, when the breeze is blowing my long, silky hair, when the birds are singing of love, when the children are playing at the beach. Sweet summer days, singing all summer long.

A cool summer sweet night on the beach, looking at the moon, while the beautiful moonlight is reflecting on the ocean with the gold, shimmering sand. A perfect view for a summer night.

Alima Khatun (10)

A Day In The Life Of A Mermaid

As I dived into the coral reef, an incredible tail appeared before my eyes, a brilliant red. A school of rainbow-coloured fish waved hello to me as they passed. The crabs started up a song and the fish started up a dance. Everything was colourful. Sharks smiled, jellyfish did the conga, dolphins drummed, corals swaying, all things bright and beautiful.

I got caught in the beat ... until I woke up on the beach with my dog licking my feet!

Danielle Pearson-Smith (11)

Monday Night

On a Monday night a small boy called David Jones lay asleep in his bed. It was a typical cold, moonlit night. The shining, bright stars were hidden behind a thick, grey blanket of clouds. He was woken by the sound of tall, bare tree branches scraping against the glass of his window.

He switched on his lamp on a side table next to his bed and listened to the frightening sounds. David stared at the blue curtain and bravely stepped out of his bed. Trembling with every step, he reached out and pulled the curtain open ...

He sighed with relief, for all he found was indeed a bare tree scraping his window. But unfortunately for David, he lived opposite an old graveyard. He looked deep into the dark, only to be terrified more. He saw a tall, slender figure carrying a sharp, shining knife, looking straight at David with a smile on his face which would send a shiver down your spine.

David stepped away from the window so he was not seen by the figure, and then he swallowed in fear ...

Charlotte Aspinall (12)

Sports Stories

One day two boys, Zack and Cody, were playing football with their friends. The score was 2-1. The boys made a deal that they would meet at the football pitch again tomorrow.

After breakfast, Zack and Cody headed over to the football pitch. The other boys weren't there. They waited for hours, but the other boys still weren't there. Suddenly, a spaceship hovered above Zack and Cody. It lifted them up and took them away to a football pitch.

When they got there, they got off and they looked around the pitch. Then some aliens came out and Zack and Cody stared longingly at them. The shortest alien said a friendly, 'Biberty bop!'

Another ship flew quickly down. Out came several arguing aliens. All around them were thousands of aliens from all different planets.

The referee blew a whistle, the football game began.

An hour later the score was 4-2. Two hours later the score was 7-5! In the final ten minutes, an alien did a nasty tackle on Cody. Oh no! A penalty was awarded. Cody scored! The crowd went wild! Out came a shiny, golden cup with some medals. The cup was given to Zack and Cody.

The aliens disappeared, the boys were back at the football pitch with their friends.

Rachel Seaton (7)

Down At The Beach

Meghan was pacing up and down the sandy beaches of Blackpool waiting for her boyfriend Michael. She waited anxiously, minute after minute. Meghan was starting to get concerned. Where is he? Where is he? Meghan then saw a black Aston Martin pull up around the corner. It was Michael.

'Where were you?'

'I lost track of time, sorry.'

They started playing in the sea, splashing and having fun. Suddenly, Meghan saw her ex-boyfriend, Aston.

'Michael, can you please go and get me a hot dog?'

'OK.'

She just wanted him to leave so her ex-boyfriend wouldn't see her with Michael. Then Meghan saw he was with another girl. She called Michael over. Meghan ate her sizzling hot dog and carried on with her day, with a horrible red sunburn and also at the beach she was scarred for life because she still had feelings for Aston.

Charlotte Mickleburgh (10)

The Mystery Boy

'Here we are,' said Mum as the girls tumbled out of the car.

Ellen went to the boot and got the food for the picnic. Finally, everything was ready. Ellen wiped her forehead with the back of her hand.

After everyone had eaten, the kids wanted to play hide-and-seek.

'I'll count to 40,' said Beth.

Ellen raced off to the bushes and came to a stone circle. Of course, she said to herself, 'Mum said we were going to Rollright stone circle.'

'Found you,' said Beth.

Ellen turned. 'You didn't count to 40!'

'I did.' Beth was gaping at something behind Ellen.

When Ellen turned she saw a boy. He had bleached blond hair, he was tall and he had blue dye on his arms and face. Ellen gasped. He looked like a Celt.

Beth asked the boy, 'Do you wanna play hide-and-seek?'

The boy looked at her blankly, but eventually he understood and he managed to play.

When they got back to the car, Ellen's curiosity got the better of her and she asked her mum, 'Who was that boy near the Rollright stones?'

'We were the only people there, dear, what do you mean?'

Camilla Radwan (10)

Mermaid Treasure

Once upon a time there was a little girl called Rosie. She was sitting on a rock looking at the sea when a stingray swam up to her and said, 'What are you doing?'

'I am bored. I want to go on an adventure,' said Rosie.

The stingray replied, 'Hop on my back and I will take you on an adventure.'

They swam past some turtles and fishes. They saw an upset mermaid who'd lost her jewellery, so Rosie said, 'We will help you find it.'

They looked at a shipwreck but got chased out by a shark! The shark had big, sharp teeth and swam fast. At one point Rosie and the stingray thought they'd lost the shark, but *snap!* went the shark's teeth. The stingray moved so fast that Rosie was falling, falling, falling. She landed on a big fish, but it swam off. She found herself falling again through a big crack in the rocks. She landed painfully on something.

When she climbed off the pile she was sitting on, she screamed with joy. 'Little mermaid,' she shouted, 'I have found your jewellery!'

Chloe Chettleburgh (7)

Magic Paper

It was the summer holidays and I was searching for my favourite game so I could play on my Xbox, but instead, I found a burnt-looking piece of paper. I carefully picked it up.

Suddenly, light was everywhere. I could only see bright yellow light. Finally, the light faded. I looked at the ground, there was the piece of burnt paper. I realised it was a map. Next to it there was a shovel, but there was something else. I was standing on a red cross, that meant there was treasure!

I began to dig with the rusty shovel, sand flicking everywhere. After ten minutes I got tired, but I kept on digging till clunk! The shovel hit a metal box, not what I thought was a treasure chest, but a big metal box. There was a big padlock on it, but I noticed that it wasn't locked. I shoved the lid back. I thought I had found gold, but there sat another burnt piece of paper.

Here's what it said:

'You have found the treasure, well the treasure is in every person who has a loving heart, someone who gives love to you and to other people'.

Benjamin Num (10)

The Horse And The Harmonica

'Yippee!' cheered Mandy Hope. 'It's nearly the summer fayre!'

Mandy Hope and her family were all very excited about the summer fayre because Mr Hope, Mandy's dad, was playing his treasured harmonica in a band. He loved playing his harmonica so much because he was very good at it and also was the leader of the group.

Mr Hope was busy practising his piece when suddenly, a very miserable man with wispy, brown hair walked in.

'Hello,' he grumbled.

Mr Hope was rather startled by the sudden noise and nearly dropped his harmonica. 'Oh ... hello,' answered Mr Hope, stuttering a little. 'How can I help you?'

'I have a very keen stallion and I was wondering if you could possibly try calming him down a little?'

'Well, I'll try my best,' said Mr Hope, a bit more confident now.

When Sam the stallion trotted in, Mr Hope was a little bit surprised at how small he was. 'Well, I think I'll be able to manage him,' reassured Mr Hope confidently with a little chuckle.

'Well, just keep an eye out, he's rather mischievous,' replied Sam's owner as he strode out of the door. He'll be easy to manage! Thought Mr Hope, but he should have listened ...

Four days later, the summer fayre arrived in the village and the Hopes were all extremely excited and thought they were well prepared. They had about half an hour until they had to set off, but Mr Hope was already flustered about his notes and tunes.

Minutes later, all you could hear was Mr Hope yelling, 'Where's my harmonica?' All the Hopes were running around the house like maniacs searching for Mr Hope's precious musical instrument. Even the animals were barking, neighing and squeaking!

'Oh no!' gasped Mandy. 'What about your band?'

'I don't know, love, just keep looking!' answered Mr Hope trying not to look worried.

Suddenly, all three of them heard a piercing whinny as if a horse was in lots of pain.

'What's that?' asked Mandy, her hands already starting to sweat.

'It must be Sam,' replied Mr Hope as he rushed into the stable.

'I think we should do an X-ray,' suggested Mrs Hope.

When Sam the stallion had his X-ray, it showed a rectangular shaped object wedged in his intestines.

'He'll need an operation to remove it,' announced Mr Hope as he pulled on his white gown and rubber gloves.

After the operation, Sam was recovering well and eating as normal, but what was the object stuck inside him? Well, that's for you to figure out!

Holly Waterworth (10)

A Twist In The Tail

The summer holidays had begun. I watched as joyous families pranced to the golden beach. I spread myself across an emerald stretch of grass. As I dozed off, a beautiful fragrance started to tug at my nose. I followed the scent. A little mouse scuttled past me. I easily became distracted.

Suddenly, I found that I was on canine territory. But before I could run, a filthy terrier snapped at my ankles. It chased me to the docks. I couldn't resist stealing a fish from the fisherman's basket. As I sped away with the fish, I heard a fisherman shout, 'Edward!' but I didn't stop. I ran up the lighthouse, leaving the dog at the bottom. Then that smell ...

I ran towards the lighthouse. The pungent terrier was gaining on me. I spied a tree. I raced towards it. I flung the fish at the dog, hitting him between the eyes. I scrambled up the tree, the dog left behind. It ambled away disconsolately. I lay along a branch, hung down a paw and a tail and miaowed, then dozed off into a sweet sleep.

I jerked awake - there was that smell again ...

Neema Mwande (11)

My Running Brother

My brother, Lewis, found out yesterday that he'd won a competition to run a marathon. So he practised all the time. He loved to run, although the marathon was tomorrow.

Lewis woke up very early that morning and he was very excited. I was also going to watch. Dad kept on saying, 'Good luck!'

Our dad took us down in the car and stayed to watch as well. So Lewis was standing on the line, then the man shouted in a microphone, 'On your marks, get set, go!'

They all started to run around the town. It took 17 minutes and we saw the first person. But was it Lewis? It was Lewis! He had come in first place in the marathon and had a big gold medal!

Kelsie King (11)

Ghost Mystery

It was after my breakfast one morning when the phone rang. It was my friend, Emily, asking if I wanted to do something and then have a sleepover. I said, 'Yes, sure.'

We had a great day painting our nails, watching films and eating sweets. Emily's dad, Simon, was setting up their huge, blue camping tent in the garden. Emily and I really wanted to sleep in it. We begged Simon to let us and he finally gave in.

Emily and I were really tired after our long day, so we went straight to bed. Suddenly, in the middle of the night, Emily and I woke up because we heard a noise. It sounded like someone was on the trampoline. Then we heard footsteps, then our zip moved up and down. We got our phones and used them as torches and shone them around our tent, but nothing was there. The noises stopped and Emily and I ran inside as fast as we could and we didn't look back.

After that, we never slept outside again!

Faye Fanthorpe (12)

The Scroll

One day, Rosie Parker was walking near the river when suddenly, a scroll came out of nowhere. Rosie picked it up. You might think there would be writing on it, but it was blank! She thought it would be best if she showed it to her mum, but to her surprise, she couldn't because when she looked up she was in a completely different place - not by the river, in the 18th century. She looked around for help, but there was nobody in the town! A town with no people!

Then, after a few minutes the scroll jumped up and unrolled itself. It said, 'If you don't get the people back here, then you will never get back to where you belong'.

Rosie was shocked. When she finished reading it, she thought and thought until *bang!* An explosion came from her left. She asked a lady in a black coat what had happened. She said, 'The chief of the town was angry so he ordered his men to destroy the town.'

Then Rosie had a plan. She shouted, 'Hey people, why don't you go back to the town you lived in before?'

Some people agreed, they were safe while the others died in pain. Rosie fortunately got back home and never told anyone what happened on that day.

Danielle Yu (10)

Faraway Treasure

Once, there was a boy called Alex. He always wished that he could go on a treasure hunt. He built a massive ship with 12 rooms in it. He got in his ship and sailed off.

On the way, he saw lots of sharks and fishes, then in the distance he saw land. 'Land ahoy!' shouted Alex.

On the island suddenly appeared pirates. One of the pirates saw Alex and took him in a room filled with crocodiles. The crocodiles came closer and closer to him, when a boy showed up and stopped the crocodiles. He threw all of them out of the room. Alex asked the boy what his name was and he replied, 'Ben Billion.'

Alex said, 'Cool name.'

Ben Billion asked Alex, 'Are you trying to find the treasure?'

Alex said, 'Yes, I am.'

Then Ben Billion said, 'I know where it is.' Ben showed him the missing treasure and gave it to him.

Alex said goodbye to Ben and sailed home with the treasure.

Ben Chick (8)

Milly's Amazing Daytrip!

As Milly lay in bed, her eyes opened to the smell of breakfast. 'Mmmm, bacon!' Milly jumped out of bed and ran downstairs.

'Morning, birthday girl!' said her mum.

While Milly was eating breakfast, her mum said, 'We have a surprise for you! We're going to the beach!'

After a while, when everyone was ready, they all went to sit in the car. Off they went! After a while Milly started to doze off - Milly was asleep!

The car went over a bump and Milly was awake! Then Dad found a parking place. He turned the engine off and they jumped out of the car. Milly said, 'Where's the beach?'

Her dad replied, 'Turn around!'

Milly turned round. The first thing she saw was the blue sea. Milly ran to the beach and quickly got changed. She ran to the sea with her pink bucket to play. She bent down to get some water. Suddenly, there was a huge shadow. Milly looked puzzled. She looked up and in front of her was an old ship. Two ugly pirates grabbed Milly and chucked her in front of the captain. The captain leant over, grabbed her shoulder and said, 'Where's Fantasy Island?'

Amy White (10)

Bones

'Final call to Rome'. Those were the words in my head when we arrived at the airport late!

We finally arrived in the busy city of Rome. The first thing on my mind was that I had to fulfil my dream of climbing a mountain, although Paris had other ideas. So we went our separate ways, Mum with Paris and Dad with me, Sky. Mum wondered why we couldn't do both, but on separate days. There was a reason, but we couldn't tell her. The thing that I hate most is ... Paris!

As I trekked up the mountain, I stumbled across something cold and stiff. I screamed. A shaking finger came across my lips from the soil beneath me. Dad was far behind and couldn't hear my echoing scream. I thought it was a dream.

His crumbling bones grabbed me by the throat. I rose well into the air. Dropped. My small fingers clenched the edge of the cascading cliff. It was too late ... I fell!

Hollie Dingley (11)

A Day At Ulgham Animal Sanctuary

One morning, my nana and granda took me to Ulgham Animal Sanctuary. When we got there, we paid and got two bags of food. We went inside an open barn. There were three goats trying to jump over the wall to get some food. My granda gave them some food and then they tried to eat the paper bag. Then we saw some chickens and some peacocks. We also saw some owls. Then we went inside a hut and looked through the glass. There was a fox lying on a piece of wood. Then outside, my grandparents sat on a wooden chair and my little brother and I went to see some sheep and goats.

When we went to the picnic tables, one of the staff brought out a real hedgehog. Then we went to the park near the tables. Chloe, my little brother's friend who was there too, pushed us on a giant swing and then my brother wanted to go on a horse. When we lined up to go on, he didn't want to go anymore. So we went home.

Susan Nelson (11)

Felix Of The Future

One night Felix was asleep and a window smashed, so he woke up his wife.

'Wake up, wake up, a window smashed from downstairs,' Felix whispered. Felix woke his children up as well. Their names were Sophie and Jake.

The family went downstairs. There was a chewed up glove and all of the dinner had gone. Then suddenly, they saw a caveman. He was under the sink. The caveman looked scared, but then Jake said, 'Don't worry, we won't hurt you.'

Felix said, 'A time machine has made the caveman come.'

'Dad, can we keep him, please?' Jake begged.

'Only for a week,' Felix said.

After a week it was time for the caveman to go. Jake taught him how to catch a ball. Felix and his family went to a field and said some goodbyes. Sophie gave him a bracelet and Jake gave him a ball. Then the caveman ran off into the woods.

On the way back they got lost, but Jake and Sophie bumped into the caveman. The caveman smelt their dad and found him.

Then Felix said, 'OK, we can keep him.'

So everyone walked to the car.

Fern Lane (8)

The Race Is On!

Cory Thumbless and his pirate crew, including Patrick the parrot, were getting ready to sail to sea.

Meanwhile, James Hook and his crew were also setting off. There was a race to Norway to find a map. This map led to treasure left by an old miner who would be 231 if he was still alive! Cory's crew were the favourites to find the map first because their journey was more straightforward.

Both crews set off and the race was on! James' crew had the first problem. They had forgotten to bring any food, so James chucked two crew members into the ocean and told them to bring back some fish!

Cory realised that they had no parrot food, so three of his crew went back to land in a dinghy.

The following morning, the steering wheel on Cory's boat snapped off. They were crashing into islands and heading the wrong way. They were miles behind James.

James arrived at Norway and found the map. It led to the South Pole.

Four years later, James' crew reached the treasure which was hidden in an igloo surrounded by penguins. Cory's crew were stranded on an island, but with plenty of parrot food!

Robert Stoyle (9)

Molly Strikes Gold!

One morning, Alice was very excited. She was going by boat to an island with her family and their dog, Molly. Alice and her brother, Robert, couldn't wait to get there.

'Oh please row faster, Dad,' begged Alice.

Some time later, Robert saw something big and brown in the water. Perhaps it was a shipwreck. He and Alice ran to look over the side. Alice was only five years old and she started to wobble. Her dad couldn't hold her and she tumbled into the water with an enormous splash! Alice couldn't swim and she was struggling. Robert dived straight in and helped Alice to the shore nearby.

Mum, Dad and Molly arrived in the rowing boat just after. They were very happy to see Alice and Robert were safe.

After a picnic on the beach, Robert and his parents swam to the wreck, while Alice and Molly watched from the shore. They saw nothing of interest and swam back to the beach, disappointed.

As they sat down, Alice saw something sparkling in the sand. Molly started digging and they soon pulled out a big chest full of gold. They went home very happy carrying Molly's treasure!

Amy Starritt (8)

Kitten Excitement

The 29th, I was so excited because at 6.30pm I was going to get two brand new kittens.

All day I was bored out of my brains waiting till 6.30pm. Me and my sister were walking up and down the road, hoping for time to pass. I sat and stared out of the window, but it made things more boring and longer. So me and my sister went and played on the swings until my mom came up the garden to tell us that the kittens had just arrived and were inside. So my sister and I leapt off the swings and dashed down the garden.

I saw them both and the excitement inside of me was unbelievable. My mum and dad had to fill in some forms and after all the forms were out of the way, we had them both to ourselves. We named them Daphne and Smudge.

Harriett Pringle (9)

Bob And The Bear's Adventure

Once upon a time there was a boy called Bob and a bear called Albert. They wanted to go on an adventure to an island.

The next day Bob asked his mom to give them both a lift in her car to the boat shop to buy a boat to travel across the sea. There were so many to choose from, but then they found just the right one. It was an engine boat.

Albert came up with a great idea. He said, 'Why don't we go on a treasure hunt too?'

When they were there, they got out their book and started their treasure hunt. They went to the first island and found a treasure map and followed the X until they came to another island and found the X. Albert dug with his long claws, then they found the chest. Inside the chest was gold, silver and money. They took the chest back home to their mum and lived happily ever after.

Nayim Miah (8)

When I Grow Up

When I grow up I want to be a champion swimmer. I would win all the medals in the world. I would be very famous and I would live in a mansion with a king-sized swimming pool. I would have to train a lot and be fit for the races. If I wasn't feeling well, I would write a letter saying 'I cannot race today, I do not feel well, yours sincerely, Shauna Toner'.

People would come from all around the world asking if they could be a professional swimmer like me.

At night if I couldn't sleep when there was a race in the morning, I'd just think about the first time I won a gold medal.

Shauna Toner (8)

At The Beach

I looked out of the window. It was a hot, sunny day. I wanted to go to the beach! I packed up my swimming costume and my spade and beach ball. I jumped in the car and we were off to the beach.

The first thing I did was jump in the water. *Splash!* Then I dug a big hole. I buried myself in it.

When I dug myself out, I played with my beach ball. I kicked it around the beach until I got tired. I sat down and had a picnic with my mum. We had some sandwiches, sweets and cherryade. It was very tasty. Then we saw the clock in the café. Oh no! It was time to go home. So then we had one more little swim in the warm sea, then we went home.

Jessica McSkimmings (10)

The Nightmare!

There it was, sitting in the corner of the room, the evil doll with black (stare you in the eye) button eyes. Also, old-fashioned, creepy clothes and shoes. She stared me straight in the eyes, then she took her first steps and launched herself on me. I screamed ... 'Argh!'

I escaped eventually. I ran down the corridor (it felt like I was running for hours) with the doll chasing me, tripping every now and then. I thought she had gone, but there she was, standing in front of me. I stopped.

She grabbed me. I yelled, 'Mum, Mum, help me! Help me now!' I yawned, extremely sleepily. I was so tired, I fell straight down. She climbed straight on top of me, opening my sleepy eyes ...

My eyes slowly opened. Where on Earth was I? Where on Earth was she? She was out of my sight for good. 'Thank goodness, I'm glad she's gone forever,' I said to myself.

I heard a loud voice. It was my mum waking me up. It was all a mysterious nightmare ... or was it?

'Mum, I had the strangest dream ever.'

'Tell me all about it.'

Bethan Shickell (11)

Who's There?

My heart was beating like a drum as my numb hand gripped the cold bronze doorknob connected to the creaky, wooden door. The full moon reflected the uneven cobbles like thousands of glinting eyes. The cold wind whipped my face and the claw-like tree branches loomed over me, ready to pounce. I was alone, with only ghosts for company.

The door creaked open as my shivering body took a step into the spooky, uneven hallway. The door shut and I heard the bolt make a slight *clink* as it moved into the lock. *No turning back now*, I thought to myself as I started to climb up the uneven staircase with the flickering candles mounted on the walls.

I froze to the spot as something caught my eye, a horrible, grotesque skeleton pinned to the wall with bugs crawling all over it! I ran as fast as I could down a deserted, arched corridor.

Would I ever see my family again, or would I be stuck here forever? Then I heard a soft, weak banging on the wall and a weak, shrill voice. I began to scream. So there was someone else in the house after all ...

Adam Toeg (11)

The Headless Pirate

It was a stormy night in Stony Wall City. Waves crashing, lights flashing, the only sound you could hear was eerie voices. Mr Huller was a pirate, his dream was to have his own pirate ship and he also wanted to take over Stone Wall City (but everyone knew that wasn't going to happen). Mr Huller was training himself to fight. Somehow he got himself into a bet. The bet was if he lost the fight then he had to give up his dream, but if he won, he took his opponent's ship. So obviously, Mr Huller was going to take chances.

'Ready, set, fight!' Both swords went flying in the air. Two seconds later they went left, right, left, right.

Suddenly, Mr Huller's head fell off, but still won like a true leader.

Nazifa Shahjahan (11)

Lune Island

Feeling the pleasant ocean breeze on my face, I sauntered down to the port. The glistening water greeted me as I sat on my favourite bench close to a boat named 'Marina Aqua'. I leant towards the water to witness a turtle surfacing. Its shell sparkled like a polished emerald.

As I reached out to touch it, I realised that I was falling ... falling. The water swallowed me up, sucking the breath out of me. I gasped for air and ... darkness. Slowly, my eyes flickered open. Was I dead? Dull, grey water licked at my legs. Surrounding me were huge palm trees. They stood watching me like evil captors.

Quaking, my legs rose and I was standing. It was then that I knew ... Lune Island. My parents had told me the terrible stories. Suddenly, I couldn't breathe and I was floating around in the air. Extraordinary colours flashed through my head ... darkness.

Seconds later, I was in the water again, sinking. My arms and legs flailed weakly. Then, as if somebody had answered my prayer, strong arms brought me to the surface. The light stung my eyes, but I could breathe. Gasping, I lay on the wooden pier. 'Thank you,' I croaked.

Anita Bayraktar (11)

Dreaming ... Wondering ...

My summer holiday was spent at home, dreaming of big cities and sandy beaches, dreaming of shopping malls and theme parks. Thinking of hot, sunny days and no more revision guides, wondering what I could be doing instead of having my head shoved into a book. Scanning the windows, gazing longingly out at the gardens below, wishing I could lose myself outside instead of finding myself inside.

Until I found a piece of paper - a competition. A piece of fun and enjoyment, a chance to tell my story.

Elena East (12)

My Summer Holiday

It was the summer holidays and I was going to camp in a camper van for the very first time. I was going to camp in a turquoise camper van for a week in Devon. I was really excited because I had never stayed in one before. I worried it would be cold in the camper van and would I like it?

When I got there and I saw it, it was bigger than I thought.

On the first day, I walked down to the beach which was about a ten minute walk. I really enjoyed walking to the beach until I remembered I'd forgotten my swimming costume and had to walk all the way back. Then I remembered there was a shop at the beach which sold swimming costumes. I sighed a big sigh and trudged back. My cousin found it funny that I got the wrong one, so when she was sunbathing I chucked a big bucket of freezing cold water over her! It was so funny, my rib cage was hurting!

By the end of the holiday I had enjoyed it so much, I wanted to go back and do everything again. But would I go back again?

Annabel Fryers (10)

My Great Grandma

My great grandma is amazing! She's 99. I know what you're thinking - she must be old and frail, but no, 'Just another number,' she says, up for anything.

All the way from Scotland she came and at the moment she's staying with us. Surviving the first and second World Wars, she never complains. My great grandma makes a house a home! She's been through the good and bad times and this year she's had her first McFlurry's ice cream.

If you see her, she looks about 79, not 99! Having a big family, her kind and loving nature shines through. My great grandma bakes lovely cakes and bread, knits pillows and jumpers and more. Always on for a day out and likes to know how we're doing at school. I already think you know, but my great grandma is number one!

Anna McKay (10)

My Special Brave Friend, Emily

I met Emily at playschool. She was a bright, chirpy three-year-old and we became good friends. Emily and I moved on to big school together and we remained friends, learning to read and write and play sports.

But when Emily was five, something bad happened. Emily became poorly and we were told it was leukaemia. We learnt it was a cancer that was in her blood. Emily wasn't at school for a very long time and spent months in hospital. Emily was very brave when she lost all her hair too.

Emily tried to be as cheerful as she could during her bone marrow transplant. We were all very happy as it had worked and Emily came back to school and things were brill.

Four years passed and Emily was a brilliant sports person. She was in the netball team and the cross country team. But then, suddenly Emily became poorly again. We found out the leukaemia had come back, but worse this time.

Emily passed away aged ten years. She is now an angel up in Heaven. I miss her every day and I will never forget my special, brave friend, Emily!

Suman Gill (11)

An Adventure On The Beach

One day I woke up and looked out of the window. I saw the sun beaming down, seagulls flying high in the air and a light breeze as I opened the caravan door. My mum came up to me and said, 'We're going to the beach!'

At the beach I went swimming to meet new people. I saw a girl so I went and asked her name.

'Jasmine,' she said, 'quickly, follow me.'

Suddenly, we were on an island. There were two chairs shaded by an umbrella. I sat on one and so did she. As quick as a flash, sharks were surrounding us. We grabbed some stones and hit the sharks until they went away. Then we swam back to safety!

What an adventure!

Lindsey McIlwaine (11)

The Tale Of Fantastic Miss Mouse

On a hill above the valley there was a giant wood. At the top of the hill there was a massive tree that touched the biggest cloud in the sky. Underneath the tree lived a family of mice, their names were Miss Mouse, Mr Mouse and their four small mice kids.

Every evening Miss Mouse would say to Mr Mouse, 'Well my darling, what shall it be tonight? A big slice of cheese from Wensleydale or a nice lot of crackers from Waferbite?

And when Mr Mouse had told her what he wanted, Miss Mouse would creep down the valley in the darkness of the night and help herself to whatever she and her family wanted.

Wensleydale and Waferbite were two rich farmers who were not very kind. They were not men who liked to give anything away and each night they would set mousetraps, hiding them in dark places somewhere on their farm, hoping to catch the mouse.

Each night, Miss Mouse went to see her friend Percy Pig. He would tell her where the traps were and in return she brought him some truffles from the forest. She was never caught and so left the farmers baffled.

Abigail Trott (11)

Daydream

One day I went to my nan's caravan and went on the beach. I sat down on the sand and as I sat there I let the sand run through my fingers. As I looked up I saw a ship, it came closer on the sand. Then pirates climbed off it, each of them carried a cutlass! Everyone ran, but my dad didn't see them. I tried to shout him, but it was too late, the pirates got us.

The pirates said, 'Get on the ship.'

Then a storm came and the ship rocked side to side while we sailed. The pirates made Dad and me do all the jobs, cooking and cleaning the decks. After I cleaned up from doing the cooking, I gave the dolphins that were swimming by us the scraps.

Soon we came to an island. The sun was shining and it was very warm. I could feel the sun burning my face and arms. The pirates made us get off the ship and start digging a big hole. After a while, we heard our spades hit something. It was a big chest. The pirates all shouted and jumped into the hole to pull the chest out. Inside the chest were jewels and gold coins. While the pirates were jumping and shouting with joy, my dad and I got out of the hole and ran down to the beach. How were we going to get home? We did not have a boat.

As we walked into the sea, the dolphins swam to us. We climbed on their backs and they swam away from the island. We could see the pirates following us in their ship and the dolphins swam faster and faster. I fell off into the water. As the water hit my face, I woke up. I had been dreaming!

After lying there for a bit, I got up and looked out at sea. My dad was walking out of the water and I could see dolphins in the distance. Had I been dreaming or not?

Sky Rowley (7)

My Mind-Blowing Adventure

One beautiful, warm, sunny day in the summer holidays, me, my friend Emma and my pet cat, Whiskers, all decided to have a day out. We all agreed on going to Whitby seaside. I asked my mummy to pack my seaside bag for me. Emma had gone to get her bag ready.

Me, Emma and Whiskers were all ready to go and have a wonderful day out, full of adventure and mischief.

We were soon at the seaside. The view was breathtaking. The sand was shining and glimmering like gold. The water was so pure, clean and sparkling, like crystals. We all couldn't wait to go paddling in the clean, clear water.

'I'm really hungry,' said Emma.

'OK, let's sit down on the sand and have our lunch.'

While we were both eating our sandwiches, Whiskers was enjoying himself playing in the crystal-clear water. Suddenly, there was a very strong gust of wind which blew Whiskers deep down into the sea.

'Oh no! What shall we do?'

Whiskers was in real trouble. He was drowning and panicking. Me and Emma both quickly dived into the crystal-clear sea. We soon got to Whiskers, but he was anxious to go very deep into the sea because he saw a light shining. So we started to explore the sea, deep under. What a magical moment we saw in the sea!

There was a huge palace which had a big courtyard. The palace was beautifully decorated with different coloured lights, crystals and gold stones on the walls. We couldn't resist it and had to go into the courtyard of the palace.

When we entered the courtyard, the queen of the palace came out to greet us all. 'Hello, how may I help you?'

We were all so shocked and were speechless. She looked stunning. Her crown was sparkling with silver diamonds, her dress had 24 carat gold gems on it.

'We're really sorry for coming into your palace but our cat, Whiskers, was drowning and we were helping him. Then we saw lights shining from your stunning palace!' we both exclaimed.

'Could you help us get onto dry land please?' I requested.

'Your wish is my command,' replied the queen. 'Before you go, I'd like you all to have lemonade and cheesy chips,' said the queen.

After enjoying our yummy snack, the queen gave a little gift to me and Emma. It was a mini treasure chest full of gold gems, rings and bracelets. She asked us both to cherish it forever and to always remember her.

Soon after giving us the present, the queen made a wish for us all to get back to dry land.

'Thank you your majesty,' we all said.

Before we knew it, we were on the sparkling sand. Finally, we made our way back home all safe and sound. We told our family about the adventure we'd had that day, the one we shall remember forever.

We all lived happily ever after.

Ayesha Ahmed (7)

The Day I Changed Forever!

I was going to the beach with my family and we had just boarded the train.

After five minutes of staring out of the window, I felt bored. My mum passed me a book about sea animals. If only I knew how important this information was going to be to me in the future! Luckily, I read it all.

When we arrived, the sun was shining and the yellow sand and blue water looked wonderful. I went exploring and came across a cave. To my amazement I could see a treasure chest. I ran over to it. It was an ancient box. I opened it and there were so many gold coins and sparkling jewels, the light almost blinded me. I didn't know it was cursed by pirates. I touched it and I felt a strange sensation. I had turned into a crab! I was shocked, then I saw my arms were now pincers!

My family came looking for me. They touched the treasure and turned into crabs too! At first we were all shocked, then I remembered the book about crab survival and we realised we could still live as a happy family on a beach holiday forever.

Neil Cifelli (8)

My Astonishing Treasure Hunt

I was sitting alone, all on my own, wondering what to do. Then I decided I needed something exciting and new.

I staggered way back to the pirate times. I fought and I won, I stabbed and I killed my way to my second location.

Brushing through tough, evergreen palm trees on a deserted island, I suddenly tripped over something brown and solid ... it was a treasure chest! I cautiously opened the lid and there sat the most fabulous laptop ever!

Now when I'm bored, I'll know what to do!

Charlotte Magee (8)

Summer With Tennis

It was a lovely, bright summer morning, the birds singing and the sun beaming off the bedroom window. There were these two girls called Melody and Rose. They got up out of bed and were very bouncy because they knew they had a big tennis match at one o'clock that day.

'Hurry up, Melody,' Rose said, 'put your crisp, white clothes out on the bed.'

'OK,' said Melody. So she did.

'Now we must go and get those gigantic rackets out of the cupboard.'

Melody and Rose played for Silloth and they were playing Chatsworth.

'Rose, we must get downstairs and have a whopping breakfast. Mum, don't forget to put plenty of drinks and bananas in.'

Their tennis match was at Silloth and their coach was the best. His name was David Wise. Melody started by playing Stella. It stood at 2-1 to Melody. There were a lot of overarm serves. The score at the finish: Melody 6-4.

Rose played Diane in the singles, winning 6-1.

Now over to the doubles. Play started. It did not go too well for Melody and Rose. They lost the doubles to Stella and Diane.

'Well, what a brilliant time we have had, Rose,' said Melody.

'Yes,' said Rose, with their singles cups in her hand.

Mary Hollick (8)

Time Travel

Once upon a time I went to the museum. While I was looking around, I saw an air raid shelter, so I climbed in. It was dark, cold and scary, so I closed my eyes. Suddenly, it started to shake! Then it was quiet. I looked outside. Where do you think I was? In World War One!

Suddenly, I heard a bomb. Bang! People were shouting, people were being killed. Then I went outside ...

'Hello,' I said to a man.

He said, 'Do you have any food?'

When I got my hand out of my pocket, there was a photo, it looked like the man. He was my grandad! I was speechless. He gave me a letter and said goodbye. I got back in the air raid shelter, then I was home.

'Olivia, Olivia, where are you?'

'I'm here. Do you want to know where I went to? World War One!'

'Liar! Liar!'

Olivia Moroney (9)

The Mystery Of The Missing Teacher

Mrs King leaned against the coach window and slowly closed her brown eyes. She was a thirty-year-old teacher who always liked to dress smartly. On the coach with her was Miss Smith, a classroom assistant, and a group of six-year-olds from St Peter's RC School.

Feeling tired, Mrs King decided to rest until they arrived at Brighton.

Ben and Jack were best friends and they were very excited about spending a day at the beach. As the coach moved closer, the beautiful view of the pier became clearer.

Mrs King woke up to the sound of excited children, eager to get off the coach.

After fifteen minutes, Mrs King and her class were walking happily along the beach. A gust of wind blew across Mrs King's face and she could smell seawater. Raising her voice, she loudly explained to the class that they would be spending one hour on the pier.

While the rest of the class quickly ran towards the pier with Miss Smith, Ben and Jack decided to go on a treasure hunt with Mrs King. Suddenly, as they walked further away from the pier, Mrs King found a big, yellow, shiny key that slowly began to glow. Nervously, she whispered, 'I wonder if this key is a magic key?' Holding the key in her hand, she carried on walking with Ben and Jack. As they walked further on, Jack was surprised to see a golden door at the end of the beach. Mrs King put the key into the lock and immediately the key began to change colour. With a gust of wind, the door opened and Mrs King vanished out of sight. The door closed and Mrs King and the key were nowhere to be seen.

Angrily, Ben and Jack banged on the door, praying for Mrs King to open the door. However, not only had Mrs King vanished, but the sound of the waves around them had disappeared too!

Were Ben and Jack ever going to see Mrs King again?

Emalya Maheswararajah (9)

A Sting In The Tale

It was a lovely day and Luke was looking forward to his hour lunch break. At one o'clock he left the office, called at the 'hole in the wall' to get some cash and made his way to the park.

As he approached a bench by the lake, he spotted a familiar old lady sitting there. He had spoken to her many times before and enjoyed listening to her stories about 'the good old days'. So he sat down beside her.

'Things ain't what they used to be,' she said. 'With all this violence and crime about.'

She was referring to a spate of armed robberies that had been committed in the area. One man had been shot for not handing over his wallet. Police had failed to find the offender.

'I know,' said Luke. 'I have just been to get some cash from the ATM, but I made sure nobody was watching.'

'Very sensible,' she said, 'you have to be careful, you cannot trust anyone these days.'

The hour passed quickly and Luke got up to leave.

'Just a minute,' said the old lady, pulling a gun from her bag and pointing it at Luke. 'Hand over your money!'

Kara Fox (12)

The Land Of Iquara

It was the summer holidays. I stepped into my garden and I was pretty sure it was different. Usually there was light oak decking with table and chairs, and then lovely green grass with Mum's petunias, all different colours, beaming in the summer sun. But instead, I saw a huge land with a glittering rainbow and leprechauns in green. There was a beautiful, white unicorn with a blue, shining mane and elves and fairies on red toadstools with white polka dots. It was extraordinary.

The beautiful unicorn approached me and said, 'I, Miss Jodie, shall be your noble steed.'

I gasped. 'You can speak! And you know my name!'

'Of course, anything is possible in Iquara,' replied my noble steed.

'But what is your name?' I asked.

'I am Derregalus, Miss Jodie.'

I was speechless.

I was introduced to everyone in Iquara and Derregalus took me to Strawberry mountains! But it was getting late and the sky turned pink with blue stars.

'I shall take you back to your abode, Miss Jodie,' said Derregalus.

'Yes, thank you. I am quite tired.'

And the enchanted creature carried me to my house garden door. I then found myself in the kitchen. I opened the back door, hoping to see the beautiful Iquara, but there was only my garden.

Had I imagined Iquara, or was it real?

Olivia Judd (12)

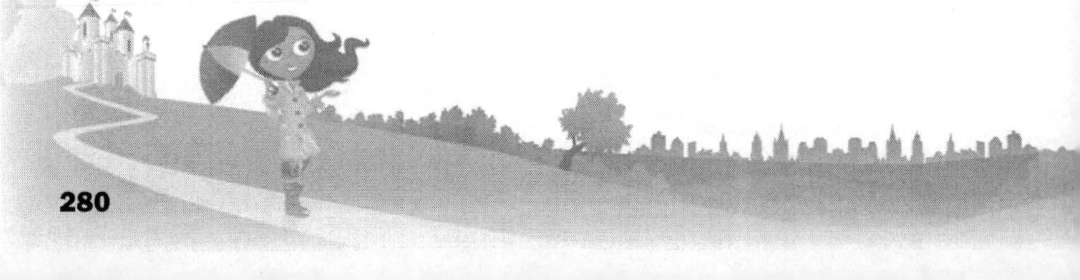

A Midnight Star

Jasmine loved to count the stars in the sky at midnight till she fell asleep! One night, she noticed a particularly big star. Suddenly, she remembered what her dad had said when she was little: ‘When you see a big star, then you know for sure that you will have a lovely dream tonight’.

Sure enough, as soon as Jasmine fell asleep, she dreamt about herself riding on the back of a snowy-white horse named Midnight Star. Jasmine had always been a horse lover, ever since she knew what they were. Now that her family had moved to a house big enough to have a horse and a stable, Jasmine begged her parents to let her keep a horse, but they always asked her to wait patiently.

On Jasmine’s fifteenth birthday, her parents let her sleep over at her best friend’s house. She had a great time!

The next day she waved goodbye to her friend. Her parents were grinning like a pair of Cheshire cats. When they arrived home, she soon realised why. She had a horse of her own! Jasmine named her new horse Midnight Star.

Joelle Phua (10)

My Summer Holiday Horror

The dark and dull door creaked open. I quickly covered my eyes. I didn't even dare to peek, but luckily I overcame my fears when I looked at the Winchester mystery house. I screamed the soul out of me ... 'Argggghhhhh!' Dead bodies, cobwebs and bloodstains splattered the wall. As I walked in I could smell a strange, dreadful smell.

As I leapt for my escape, the doors slammed shut right into my face. I had to get out of here, I had to get out of here as soon as possible, even if it took 1,000 years I had to battle my way out of here.

Day by day I was one step closer to escaping from this horrifying place. Finally, I got to this huge door, slowly opened it and saw freedom. I leapt out for freedom and quickly but carefully climbed up the spiky, prickly, rusty and massive gate.

It took ages getting a taxi that dropped me off at the airport. Finally, I got a taxi to the airport and caught a flight to England and headed straight to my wonderful home.

Sorry, got to go now, the candle's burning out ...

Fiza Jamil (10)

A Rainy Day

It was a rainy day in the summer holidays, so I couldn't go out and play with my friends. There was nothing to do because the power was down.
I thought hard and then I had a brainwave.

'I've got an idea!' I said. 'I'll get all of the pillows in the house and all the blankets together and make the biggest fort you have ever seen.'

After I changed it and made it better, I got some books and games and put them in the fort in the little secret place I made. Then my cat, Jeffery, came in and wrecked the secret place, so I had to make a new one. Then I got my world record book and started to flick through it. I came across a record for the biggest pillow fort and I had beaten it. Mine was six inches bigger.

So the next day I started writing my letter to them. I got an envelope and second-class stamp and sent it off.

The following Monday I had a letter back and it read: 'Dear Megan Clarke, you have broken the world record for the biggest fort. I am congratulating you on the world record you broke. Your name and picture will be in 2011's World Record book.'

And that's how I had the 2011's World Record book that next Christmas.
I was practically famous!

Megan Clarke (10)

Being Me

Being me isn't easy, but most people would think that me being who I am, my life is a doddle. Well, think again! I've got as many things to worry about as the humans have. Don't believe me? Well then, I'd better tell you.

Firstly, I have to go all round the world trying to find a place that the humans don't inhabit (which is almost impossible). Secondly, I have to wait until midnight until I can find food that I like. Thirdly, I have to live my life without anybody seeing me. Why? you ask. Well, I am Pegasus, the flying horse.

Tia Saunders (11)

The Dragon's Key

Sapphire stumbled down a dark alley, tripping over stones as she went.

'Oh, this is hopeless. How will I ever find my mum now?' she cried.

Sapphire and her mum had been shopping at the market and the next thing she knew, her mum had gone! As she sat down on the ground, tears sprung from her bright, green eyes.

'Maybe I can help you?'

Sapphire looked up, then gasped. There, right in front of her, was a fairy! 'I've lost my key to fairy land. I can't get back without it, so if you help me, I'll send you back to your mum. My name's Azure,' the fairy told her.

'How do I help you?' asked Sapphire.

'By getting past the dragon!' replied Azure.

Suddenly, Sapphire found herself staring at a green dragon who was holding the key! She reached for the key and the dragon let out a blast of fire! Sapphire smiled and started tickling the dragon, who dropped the key. She leaned forward and ...

'Yes, I've got it!' she cried.

Sapphire handed it to Azure who clicked her fingers. She blinked and there was Mum! If only Mum knew what had happened!

Abigail Sims (10)

Beware

I was truly bored, with nothing fun to do,
So I went on a picnic, with Mum, Dad and Sue.
Us kids went to a castle, it said, 'Please keep out',
But we were dumb and went in, when I suddenly heard a shout.
The door snapped shut behind us, blocking the summer sun,
I wish we'd gone to Disney Land, or somewhere much more fun!
Well, Sue began her crying, so escaping was up to me,
If only I had a map to help me and Sue flee!
We scurried around in darkness, scared beyond belief,
When we passed a girl with hair just like a coral reef.
She looked oddly pale, I wondered was she ill?
When suddenly, she ambushed us and gave us lots of pills!
When I awoke, I was tied up to a creaky seat,
So was Sue, when the girl appeared, looking eerily neat.
I noted she was translucent, surely a trick or cheat?
It seriously didn't look like she was playing fair,
Since she was free and we were sat here, tied up to a chair.
And then she spoke her only word and didn't flinch a hair,
The only word she ever said as she whispered, 'Beware!'

Molly Royle (11)

The Boring Island And The Adventure

I thought rowing in my petite boat to a deserted island in the middle of the Octavis Ocean would be fun. I was wrong! It was my last day on the island and all I'd done while being there was eat berries, drink coconut milk, climb trees and sleep. I had an inkling that my last day would be no different from the rest, but something happened to make it a little more exciting ...

I awoke that day to find a ship next to my boat. I walked towards it and I glimpsed footprints leading towards a little hut. I peered in and I saw a giant sack that was tied with a long rope. I crouched beside it and carefully unwound the rope. There were 12 objects in it. I pulled one out. It was an undersized Beagle puppy.

Suddenly, three men entered the hut and snatched the puppy from me. I yelled, 'What are you doing with these puppies?'

'Kidnapping them!' they replied.

I grabbed the long rope, tied up the men, gathered the puppies and ran to my boat!

Fortunately, the puppies were returned to their owners, but unfortunately, that is where my adventure ends.

Megan McKee (11)

What A Start!

I'm so excited! My bags are packed and I'm ready to go on holiday today! Me, Mum, Dad and my brother, Jake, are getting into the taxi to go to the airport. We're driving and I'm listening to my favourite song. Then Dad realises he's left Jake's passport behind! So we go back and get it!

Finally, we are back on the road, cruising along the motorway through the typical English rain. Cannot wait to get in the sun!

Yay, we are at the airport now! We have just checked in the suitcases. Mum's was over the weight limit! Probably filled to the brim with all her lotions and potions! Poor Dad has to pay £90 for excess luggage! At least we are through the gates now and I can't wait. Oh no! We have looked at the TV schedule and our six-hour flight to Egypt has a ten-hour delay! This is turning out to be a nightmare! Surely it can't get any worse than this, or can it?

Amy Battinson (11)

The Hammock

The summer holidays had started. I was lying on the hammock, down the bottom of the garden, strung between two trees.

Suddenly, *bang!* The cannon went and splashed in the water. The cannon landed, we all got drenched. I stood up slowly and looked around. Then I realised I was on a ship! I looked up and what I saw was unreal - a flag with skull and crossbones, which meant only one thing - I was on a pirate ship. I was shaking like a rattle. I had to make a quick escape, so I thought and thought till my brain was about to explode, then the best idea came to me ...

To climb to the top of the flagpole, jump off and swim, because I could see land not that far away. So I crept to the flagpole and climbed. Then I heard a voice getting louder and louder. I was about halfway and then I felt a tugging at my waist. I got pulled down and got put on the plank.

He shouted, 'Walk!'

I jumped in and got soaking wet ...

Then I woke up and my dad was flicking me with water!

Rhea Dickman (11)

Letters

I'm Elsie, I'm 12. Mommy just got the letter. I hate letters; they always bring bad news, since that stupid letter we got on the 23rd of October 1943. That was Saturday; I'd been counting the days. Until the second letter.

It was Saturday morning and I was lying in bed under my quilt. I knew Mom would get annoyed I was sleeping in; Saturday was my day to tend to the tomatoes. I hate tomatoes almost as much as Adolf Hitler, except our tomatoes have never been known to start a war. I heard the doorbell ring and by the way Mom likes to chat, I knew I had a bit longer in bed. Then I heard Mom crying and Dad trying to comfort her.

It wasn't until the next day at Sunday dinner that we heard about the letter. Daddy had been called to war. I didn't know what to do or say. I was the oldest of three, so I knew I couldn't cry.

Five days later, Daddy had gone. Mommy wasn't coping, we were poor. But then one day as I was lying in bed, we got another letter. Daddy wasn't coming back, ever.

Sophie Kettle Smith (12)

Pink Bikini Attack

A god sat in the summer sun,
He said, 'I'm bored, this isn't fun!'
And then he clapped his hands with glee,
'I'll make those mortals lightning tea!'

So we down here all got singed lips,
and the god settled down to eat chocolate chips.
We mortals vowed we'd plot a plan,
Against that cheeky, godly man.

The chief got out his swimming trunks,
And tied them to a stick.
'Attack!' he cried, 'And make it quick!'
'Sorry!' us mortals said, 'We're napping in our bunks.'

We hit the god with pink bikinis,
Shells and rough, gold sand,
Seawater and a wooden hand,
Even some glasses of freezing Martini!

And that god he slumped back home,
To pay for us mortals to pay for a phone.
He moaned, 'Blasted mortals, it's just a joke!'
And some big, green frogs gave a little croak.

Julia Trier (8)

Adventure At The Theme Park

It was our turn to go on 'Oblivion' at Alton Towers. We got in the back seat and the ride started. We were near the drop when our car broke off from the rest; zoomed down the drop really fast, then took us to a magic land. Suddenly, out of the blue came 'Terrawoman', a cross between a pterodactyl and a woman. It snatched my mum away and flew her across a desert. We ran across the desert passing lots of talking cacti. They told us the way to go.

We came to a river where we saw a unicorn; it was our only hope of crossing. I remembered I had mints in my pocket and unicorns love mints. We gave him two and he carried us over. We reached the 'Terrawoman's' cave where my mum was locked in a cage. We found the key and got her out.

Suddenly, the car of Oblivion appeared; we jumped in and zoomed away, finally arriving back at Alton Towers where we rejoined the rest of the ride. The ride finished and we quickly got off. We decided never to go on the back seats again!

Erin Smith (8)

The Assassin

Her horse moved with deadly silence, the darkness a cloak of death. A sudden gust of wind blew the hood back from her head. In what little light there was, it revealed a ghoulish face. Ribbons of long, black hair fluttered, their curls like ripples on water. Green eyes penetrated the darkness and a small mouth held a grim expression. At her waist something slender and sharp flashed, reflecting the moonlight on its surface.

The hood was then hastily yanked into place and the black, sleek horse was urged on into a prompt gallop, hooves thudding softly on the grass.

Approximately five minutes later, a manor came into sight and at the sight of it, the girl tensed so violently, her poor horse reared so high it almost toppled over.

Even before her horse landed, she was on the gravel of a posh drive. Her teeth were bared as she made her way to the door of the mansion in front of her. Her hand gripped the hilt of her glittery object. She then drew it, and revealed that it was in fact a sabre. The oak doors of the mansion opened and a man's scream echoed in the barren wilderness.

Freya Hulbert (11)

My Place ...

The park was my life ... I had everything there; the swings, the slide and most importantly, the giant muddy hole. I would sleep on the slide where in daytime people would laugh at me and just stand there and stare at me. They didn't know me or what it was like to live at a local park. I was abandoned by my own family, they just walked right out on me, so now I don't know who my family are, or where they are.

It was half-past one in the morning, I knew I had to go to sleep but the other day someone said something to me and they've just freaked the life out of me. I stepped into the giant muddy hole. Everybody was looking strangely at me, then suddenly a little girl said, 'Don't ever go back to your past or race to the future or the past will haunt you!'

As soon as she said that, I heard a ghostly voice whisper into my ear saying, 'Follow me, I will take you to your birth mother.'

What did this mean? Who's my birth mother?

Ah Mei Ho Knit Chong (12)

Beggar's Wings

The man sat at the corner of the street, silent. He was dressed in a thick overcoat and his hair fell madly over his wet face. People passed by him, oblivious, often walking up to him only to veer off suddenly around him, their faces in shock. His hat lay upturned by his feet, empty save one lone spider and a copper button. He gave a small sigh and reached into his pocket, drawing out a small letter. It was dog-eared and nearly destroyed, but the man read through it anyway, tears blending with the rain falling from the sky.

At his side suddenly appeared what seemed to be a person, but it was so heavily disguised in thick light, not much could be seen of the figure. Large, white wings came out from its back and it said slowly, savouring the moment, 'I think you have waited quite long enough now, Burke.'

The man looked up at the figure beside him and he seemed all of a sudden small and frail. 'Not long enough, sir.'

The figure seemed to smile. 'I know.'

Then the street corner was empty, people passing by and the rain falling hard on their heads.

Caleb Rowan (13)

The Great Mountain Adventure!

Dan and Sam were hurriedly packing for their exciting adventure up on the massive, icy Monty mountain.

At his house, Dan was carefully checking items off on his list, packing important things for the trip that would keep him and his friend safe. Things like strong rope, map, compass, energy-giving food, warm clothing, fully charged phone and a loud whistle.

Meanwhile, Sam was at his flat throwing some of his favourite things into his tatty, black rucksack that he really didn't need. Things like a well-loved, worn teddy bear, a super-sized water gun, a tub of caramel ice cream and a pair of designer black sunglasses!

The adventurers were due to meet at the foot of Mount Monty at 10.30am on 21st April. Of course, Dan arrived at 10.15am, giving him enough time to check the light and weather forecast for the day.

'Where is that Sam?' Dan asked himself when his friend had still not arrived at 11.00am!

Sam eventually arrived at 11.15am, looking like he had just crawled out of bed. His clothes were all crumpled and his hair was sticking out like the leaves at the top of a pineapple!

'Sorry I'm late,' yawned Sam, 'I couldn't get out of bed. I was at a great party last night and I didn't get home until 12.30am.'

Dan rolled his eyes but didn't say anything because he forgave his friend and just wanted to get started on their adventure. 'Come on,' he said, 'let's get started!'

Sam strolled off up the mountain alone, without knowing where he was going. Soon Dan spotted him and shouted, 'Wait Sam, you don't know where you are going! We need to follow the map or we will get lost!'

Sam walked slowly back to Dan and grinned. 'Oh, don't be silly Dan, we don't need a map because all we have to do is walk up this silly mountain and back down again. It's easy peasy!'

Dan stared at Sam and tutted. 'Oh Sam, it's not like that. It's much harder than that. It's foggy up in the mountains, so we can't see where we're going.'

Sam started to look very puzzled. 'Wait a second,' he said, 'if it's so foggy, you wouldn't be able to see the map that well, would you?'

'That's why we brought the compass, Sam,' Dan answered. 'Now come on, let's start climbing.'

Dan and Sam started to walk a little way on the journey, but unfortunately, Sam started to mumble, 'Tired, too tired, got to stop, need a rest now!' So Sam and Dan stopped off for a little rest to have their lunch.

'So what have you got in your sandwich today, Sam?' Dan asked.

'Oh, I haven't got a sandwich, I've got some ice cream!' smiled Sam.

Dan looked amazed. 'Sam, ice cream will have melted by now! That won't give you energy either. You really need to be more prepared.'

'It won't have melted,' Sam said. Sam opened his cold ice cream tub and peeped inside. 'Oh no! It's melted!' Sam cried.

'Oh, don't worry, you can have one of my sandwiches, I have brought more than enough.'

'Oh thanks,' replied Sam in an embarrassed voice.

So the boys ate their food in record time and soon they were ready to finish their trip.

'Before we finish, we need to have a drink. Have you got your water, Sam?' Dan asked.

'Yep, I've got my water!' Sam then took out the giant water gun from his rucksack and squirted some water into his mouth! Then he got really silly and started squirting water everywhere!

'Come on Sam, put that away and let's continue this adventure.' By that time, Dan began to wonder why he had ever asked Sam if he wanted to come along!

So the boys carried on with their adventure without too much trouble. Sam was beginning to realise that he should listen more to Dan - he seemed to know exactly what he was doing.

They had just about reached the top when suddenly they heard the horrible screeching noise of a whistle being blown six times.

'Oh no, Sam, someone's in terrible danger. That's the sign for someone in trouble! Quick, we need to find that person and help them,' shouted Dan.

Soon, the boys found a young girl who was in danger. Her leg was stuck under a big, grey boulder.

'Quick Sam, use your phone to call the ambulance while I look after the girl.' Dan knelt down beside the girl and assured her that she would be alright.

'Oh no, my phone isn't charged, it won't work!' Sam yelled.

'Oh Sam, don't worry, use mine, it is in the pocket of my rucksack.'

Dan took off his woolly blue scarf and carefully wrapped it around the little girl so it kept her warm whilst the air ambulance came. Of course, Dan needed to give the map reference as Sam couldn't read a map!

Finally, the ambulance arrived and the girl was carried to safety. The doctors thanked Dan for looking after her so well and left in a hurry for the hospital.

'Well done, Sam. You did well then, but you haven't been brilliantly prepared for this trip have you?'

'I know! You did well too and I promise that next time I will be more prepared for things,' promised Sam. 'Can I suggest that we take a cable car ride to the bottom of the mountain? I've had enough excitement for today!' Sam stated.

'Good idea,' replied Dan. 'I don't need anymore excitement either!'

And from that day forward, Sam has been more prepared for everything - although he does take his teddy and water gun everywhere!

Megan Berry (9)

Shark Attack

Deep down at the bottom of the sea lived five not very clever mermaids.

One day, they all went to play with the starfish in the rock pools by the beach. Eleanor, the oldest mermaid, said, 'It is getting dark, we'd best get home quickly.'

So they all started to swim back. Eleanor saw a very big shark swimming behind them and told the rest of the mermaids to swim faster and faster. They went so fast they got caught in a large fishing net and could not get out.

The shark, who was called Zac, tried ripping the net with his big, white teeth, but the net was too strong for him. The five mermaids screamed and cried very, very loudly, so loudly that they frightened Zac the shark away.

The five not so clever mermaids were still trapped inside the net. Then they saw a dolphin called Evie swimming around them. She untied the top of the net with her long dolphin nose. The five not very clever mermaids said thank you to Evie for setting them free and said goodbye to her. The five mermaids then swam home very slowly.

Amber Tattersall (6)

Tom And Takkan The Alien

One day Tom came back from school and watched some TV. Tom's sister, Amy, was upstairs looking at her tattoo. Suddenly, a hand reached out and took Tom into the TV.

'Aarrgghh!' screeched Tom.

'No need to scream human being, I will not hurt you,' said Takkan the alien. 'I am Takkan, what's your name?'

Tom didn't know what to say because he couldn't stop looking at Takkan's abnormally large head. He eventually said, 'I'm Tom. Why have you brought me here?'

'Because I have to give a human being powers. So what powers would you like?' asked Takkan.

'Speed!' exclaimed Tom excitedly.

'Very well,' said Takkan.

The next day Tom walked to school. He got there really early and started to play football with some other kids. When Tom got the ball, he ran to the other team's net. Suddenly, Tom fell and everybody laughed. For the rest of the day, Tom didn't talk to anyone. When he went home he watched TV and the hand came again.

'What would you like now?' asked Takkan.

'Super strength!' screamed Tom happily.

When Tom woke up the next day, he felt strong. As soon as he finished brushing his teeth, his toothbrush broke. Oh well, he thought. When he was changed and had eaten, he set off for school. At break time Tom leaned against a tree and the tree fell down and cut all the electricity wires. He knew he was going to be in trouble, so he ran home.

When he got there, his sister, Amy, was watching TV. She didn't notice he was home early. Then the hand came.

'Aaarrrggghhh!' screamed Amy.

'Don't scream,' said Tom.

'Hello Tom,' said Takkan, 'what would you like today?'

'Nothing. I just want my nails to taste of broccoli so I don't bite them,' replied Tom.

'And I want my tattoo to come off,' said Amy.

'OK,' said Takkan.

The next thing Tom knew, he was at home. He tasted his nails. 'Ugh!' he said.

Noor-Un-Nisa Fatima (10)

Mission To Mars

My name is Elise, I am seven years old and I live in a big house in the countryside. Every night in bed, just before I go to sleep, I see flashing lights in the sky, but my mum always tells me it's just the stars twinkling.

One morning, I went to play in the fields behind my house. As I kicked my football, I noticed a large shadow on the ground. I looked up to see a spaceship the size of an aeroplane floating above my head! I was that frightened, I could not speak. Then a large door opened and a giant staircase dropped down. Three little green aliens appeared. One of them said, 'Hello,' and asked my name.

I replied, 'Elise.'

They told me they were from the planet Zog and needed to get to the red planet, Mars, but had run out of food and water. They needed my help, so I ran home, grabbed a bag, filled it with food and drink from my fridge and took it to them.

They thanked me, said goodbye and told me the flashing lights in the sky at night was them travelling the solar system.

Elise Tattersall (7)

A Relaxing Summer!

It all starts with finishing school, no more work, just a relaxing six weeks. You can always make the most out of this holiday, the sun is always out, the cold days never exist.

A famous thing about the summer is none other than spending masses of time at the beach, always waiting for the sun's arrival. Sandcastles, sunbathing and the cool sea breeze make this place a most fun and relaxing place to be.

But it's always okay to spend time inside, but that will probably be when you need a short break!

There's always a way to enjoy your summer, but make sure you have plenty of suncream with you because you're going to be facing some hot weather.

Do you have a way of enjoying your summer? Everyone always has ways of enjoying theirs.

Your animals can make the most out of their summer too. You can play with them when you have free time.

So what's the most fun season? Summer is! No argument!

Ryan Tanner (11)

Double O Nothing

The name's Jones, David Jones! I repeat the line several times in my head. If only I was able to say that line out loud one day. I realise it might be a long time before that happens!

I breathed in a large gulp of air, then let it out again with a tremendous sigh. If only my life wasn't so boring. If only I could run around, a 3.495 double range pistol in my sweaty palm as a super weird maniac chases me through the crowded streets of London! Of course, I know it will never happen, but it's worth thinking about!

I start imagining running along in the jungle, the mad man, Haden, chasing after me. I run and run, my flowing cape trailing along behind me. I realise I'm running around the snug, a tattered old rug hanging from my shoulders. I hop onto the sofa and feel the springs bouncing up and down under me. I think for a minute.

I know I'll never be a proper spy like Johnny English or James Bond, but at least I have my imagination to help me through life. Wow! Now that's a happy ending.

Georgina Fiennes (11)

Murderer

My mind was a blur, everything around me changed, one minute I was with my friend, the next lying in hospital close to my death. Doctors were telling me I'd die any day, any night. Police were questioning how I ended up here; I couldn't remember.

I felt myself slowly fade, and as I did it came back to me how it happened. I was crossing the road with my friend; I saw a man watching me but didn't know what he wanted. I stayed calm but it turned out he wanted me dead.

I have come for my revenge, you killed me for no reason. I will haunt you till you can take no more, I will make you regret everything you did and I will play tricks on your mind. The only person who will see me is the person I last saw.

'Jessica, Jessica!' I heard you shout, how did you know my name?

I carried on watching you. But then I saw you pull out a book of me; it had pictures of me that I don't remember. The one thing I didn't get is that I never saw you! You were my stalker!

Molly Ripley (11)

A Dog's Life

One bright morning Jessi was going to get a dog from the dog shelter!

At last, Jessi was at the shelter and there were 63 dogs! At first she couldn't decide but then a dog called Mogo struck her eye. He was a chocolate Labrador, he had the cutest face! That day Jessi and Mogo had so much fun and Mogo was fine at night! They made a perfect pair!

Later in Mogo's life, when he was seven, he did something amazing! When Jessi was walking Mogo by the river she let him off the lead for a swim when suddenly *splash!* Jessi fell in, Mogo was already in so he lunged forwards and grabbed Jessi with his paws and he swam back to the shore with Jessi!

The next day Mogo took the front page of the newspaper in big bold words it said: *Pooch Saves Lovely Lady!* And there was a picture too, Jessi was so proud of Mogo!

They were in more newspapers and they moved to Hollywood and met TV stars! Jessi got married and had a baby! Mogo had puppies too!

Rebecca Greensmith (8)

What Scares You The Most? Washing!

Mum was never an early bird except for the day I had my sleepover, she got up to wash pots, hang washing, hoover the rooms, open windows to air them and move the cat in the spare room, it was timid.

When my friends arrived we had fun before Mum did spaghetti Bolognese for tea.

We decided to sleep in the garden; later we were telling stories in the tent, when we heard a scratching. I got the torch to see if I could see anything.

Looking round the garden I saw a pair of legs walking back and forth with no body. We all screamed. The scratching got louder. With that we ran into the house and into Mum who we'd woken up. 'What's the problem?' Mum asked. We told her about the scratching and the walking legs. Mum laughed and said, 'You're so funny.' I asked what it was outside but Mum kept laughing and told us the walking legs were my jeans she'd washed and left out; the scratching was the cat trying to get in as it had escaped through the open window and was scared of our screaming!

Ashleigh Bowles (11)

Everyday Fun

One sunny afternoon, when the children were at the beach, they found a treasure map that showed they were in the very spot where the treasure was buried. They looked everywhere but they could not find it. Then they saw a cliff. When Sophie started to climb it the others followed her up. Josh slipped and fell but he grabbed onto a stone and started to climb back up and they carried on going up the rocky mountain.

Then they reached the top and went looking again. They did not find anything there but an old pirate flag. Sophie had an idea, she said that the flag might be where the treasure is.

'Max where did you find the flag?'

'Over there by that tree,' he said.

Sophie went there and started to dig but still didn't find anything there. So they climbed back down and kept on searching the beach. Then they saw a palm tree and started to dig together and found a trunk full of gold and a note saying: 'You have worked as a team. When someone fell you helped them up. Well done. Signed: Peg-Legged Boris'!

Émer Thompson (8)

My Alien Abduction

One night when I was sleeping, aliens invaded my house, they abducted me. I didn't know where I was when I woke up. I was attached to a noisy machine like something you'd see in Doctor Who! I later discovered that the aliens were called Bowser and Banger from the planet Zing Zong.

I called for help but no one could hear me, I was in space! As if by luck there was suddenly a huge crash at the side of the ship. Banger went to investigate and Bowser stayed with me so I couldn't escape. *What would my mum do if she was here?* I thought, *my mum would make a deal.*

I was about to start to try when my mum barged in. (She'd made herself a spaceship, only my mum could, but she was not the best at landing!) With Banger demanding my release, I told them that between my mum and me we could teach them everything they wanted to know and we'd show them all different kinds of human activities and in return they agreed to teach us about aliens.

My mum and I returned to Earth so excited about our future adventures with Bowser and Banger!

Molly Price (8)

Jamie's Surprise

Once there lived a little girl called Jamie. She was very excited because it would soon be her birthday. On her birthday list she said she wanted a guitar, a poster of her favourite pop star and a book. She heard her mum arranging something, but what? What she did hear was that her new neighbours, Danny and Lucy were coming over.

That night was the night before her birthday. The next morning she woke to the sound of people singing happy birthday to her. So she went downstairs to open the presents. She got a guitar, the poster that she wanted and a book. She asked if she could go to play with Danny and Lucy. 'Yes,' said Mum. When Jamie was out Mum and Dad started blowing up balloons. What were they up to?

They played hide-and-seek. Jamie was seeking, but she couldn't find them anywhere. So she looked in the house. 'Oh!' she said, 'it's very dark in here.' She turned on the light.

'Surprise!' everyone shouted. It was her very own surprise party. They all had a great time singing and playing games. Where were the friends hiding though? That will remain a secret.

Emily Nix (8)

The Dream

It began on a cool, breezy summer morning …

'Mum are we going to the beach?' I asked.

'Yes, just give me five more minutes,' she replied.

'You said that twenty minutes ago.'

(We were meant to have left an hour ago but she's always too busy doing her precious hair.)

An hour later

We finally arrive at the sandy beach. As Mum finds a place to sit and relax, my sight is drawn to the sea which glistens in the sun like a crystal. I show Mum. I can tell by the look on her face that she is amazed by the beautiful sight.

Suddenly the warm sun vanishes and is replaced by a blinding flash of lightning. Everybody screams while taking cover. Mum and I run away, petrified. I collapse after falling over a rock. Patterns whirl around in my head. Colours of pink, blue, purple and red.

I wake up on a train after falling asleep. Turns out it was all a dream. I realise I'm on the train because we're on our way to Barry Island beach. The mystery is waiting for me. Could it really become a true tale? Who knows …

Megan Davies (11)

The Eyes

As I leant out of the balcony, staring at the pretty flowers, I felt like somebody or something was watching me. I cautiously peered around but saw nothing. I glanced back at the flower, then, in the middle of the roses, spotted a pair of gleaming green eyes, staring at me. I had no idea what it could be, but my best bet was to follow them. It was a reasonable distance between me and the fence. I stood on the rail of the balcony and made a petrifying leap towards the fence. It shook but somehow I managed to grab on with one hand and pull myself up onto the thin ridge. As I wobbled myself beyond the flowers and balanced past the bracken, the eyes disappeared up a tree. Unfortunately it was so dark I could hardly see, but I was determined to try! I began to climb, I got scratched and cut but I made it eventually! I got close enough to see the eyes gleaming as bright as the sun. I could see the black hairs, the pointy ears, the furry tail. I had risked my life to follow a cat!

Maja Pegler (10)

The Rainy Day Box

Emma sat grumpily on her window seat, watching the lashing rain through the cracked window in her bedroom. Emma was about to fall asleep, when Katy and Jo lounged in. 'What do you want?' Emma enquired.

'I just wanted you to come up into the loft with us,' replied Katy.

'Sure,' replied Emma.

The three girls climbed up the stairs and halted at the door. 'Right Emma you wait here while Jo and I root around.'

'Oh brill!' snapped Emma.

'Well we are in danger up here,' Jo whispered sheepishly.

'Oh go away, I have got the point!' shouted Emma.

Katy and Jo walked into the dark, gloomy loft and left Emma with nothing else to do but watch the spiders scuttle around the dusty corners. At last they emerged through the darkness clutching an old box.

They retreated and left the musty smell behind but brought the unsettling sensation with them. They reached the lounge, prised open the lid and peered inside. It was littered with cobwebs and was filled with books, games and magazines. The girls were hypnotised by the box and didn't look up when the sun finally shone through its cloudy enclosure.

Carrie-Anne Griffin (11)

The Day I Left The Earth

It was Saturday evening at Devonshire cottage and Taylor was trying to get a high score in her favourite ever game on the computer. In the blink of an eye something was in the corner of the screen. Taylor paused it to read what the note said: 'Once you read this there's no turning back. A girl the age of 8 was murdered in 1945; her body was found washed up on a lake bank in 1947. Tonight at the strike of 12 the girl will jump out of your wardrobe and haunt you. To prevent this put in your room one perfume bottle.'

That night Taylor forgot to prevent it … at the stroke of 12 the girl appeared …

Ruth Dent (10)

Piranha Attack

It happened two weeks before the end of Year 6. We went to the Robinwood Activity centre for three days; only to find that our first activity was 'piranha pool'.

We were told we had 45 minutes to retrieve the key for the sealed door, before the piranhas were released into the pool. The intelligent piranhas could sense that we were nearby and would jump out of the water as an effort to try and nibble on us. The staff couldn't remove their teeth because the RSPCA thought that was animal cruelty; thus we were liable to being bitten.

We entered the room, having to complete a series of puzzles and challenges that enabled us to use the equipment around us, like 'the swing of no return'.

With only three minutes left, our entire group was on the opposite side that we started on. We were time conscious and had to use the slippery pole to get to the door. Everyone fled down the pole, falling into the pool as a result. The last set of people ran for their lives … the piranhas had been released!

Oore Akinosun (11)

The Star

Eight-year-old Olivia Stoner sat opposite her aunt Marian, bored rigid. She had to admit that it was nice of Marian to look after her while her parents were ill, but this 'fun trip' wasn't the least bit fun. It was only after a moment of staring blankly around the deserted carriage that Olivia realised something peculiar on her aunt's right hand. A star, tattooed between her thumb and index finger. She barely had time to open her mouth and ask before the train shuddered to a stop.

'This is us,' Marian said, taking Olivia gently by the hand onto the platform. The train pulled away into the darkness, leaving a lightless station basking in gloom. Olivia looked around with wide, hazel eyes and held herself closer to Marian. No one was there and there wasn't a sound to be heard anywhere.

'Stay here for a moment sweetie,' Marian said, and swept out of sight. Olivia stayed absolutely still shuddering as a sudden rush of cold air ran down her spine. Then she heard a voice, her auntie's voice, 'That's her.'

'Auntie?'

Silence.

And then from out of the shadows they came …

Naima Heath (9)

The Baby Bird

One rainy morning I put my clothes on and went for a little walk. On the way I saw a baby bird. His feathers were wet so he could not fly. I decided to put him in a cardboard box and set off home.

I dried his wings gently with a red towel. I went out into the garden and pulled up a couple of tasty, juicy worms and picked some fresh leaves and twigs for his nest. The little bird made a nest from the leaves and twigs and ate the juicy worms hungrily.

The next morning the little bird was cheeping merrily and completely dry. I opened the door and he flew up in the air and landed on my arm. I thought I would call him Chirpy.

From that day on the little bird would often sit on my window ledge saying, 'Chirpy, chirpy, who's a pretty boy.'

Jemma Ellis (7)

My Roasting Summer

For me summer is just a great, big fun opportunity, that is why this summer will be one I will never forget.

It all started when my brother and I were playing hide-and-seek for the twenty-seventh time. We had hidden in every hiding spot in my house. There was nowhere left to hide. All except the forbidden room. Would I risk those weeks I'd be grounded? Yes! I grabbed the key and unlocked the old, rusty door. I slowly pushed it open to find myself standing on bleached, white sand. I took one step forward and stopped. It was silent. I was going to shout, but I didn't. The beach seemed nice at first - so I sat down.

All of a sudden, a bottle washed ashore. A note inside read: 'Help me'. I looked around to find a man, no, a Prince, tied to a rock with seaweed. I ran as fast as I could and cut him free. I asked him who tied him up. He answered, 'The dragon.'

I turned round and there it was, breathing fire. We quickly covered our faces.

When I next dared to look, I was back in my room, with the Prince!

Alice Relton (10)

The Magic Compass

It was a rainy day - I was bored. That was until I went into the attic and found an old compass with a note which said, 'This compass can take you anywhere you wish to go'. I had always wanted to be a diver so I said, 'Under the sea.' Immediately, I was dragged through a portal and found myself in diving gear swimming in the sea! I was surrounded by beautiful fish and fantastic sea creatures.

Suddenly I felt something clinging to my leg; I was hurled upwards and came face to face with a giant crab! I didn't want to be eaten so I quickly whispered to the compass, 'The Pyramids of Giza.'

I was sucked into the portal and found myself in the Pharaoh's tomb itself! I began to stuff my pockets with gold, but a loud creaking made me turn around and there was a mummy! It grabbed my arm and began absorbing my blood! I screamed to the compass, 'Where I feel safe!' - and found myself back home.

The gold in my pockets had vanished, but I still had the compass!

Now I can't wait for the next rainy day - it certainly won't be boring!

Emily Lampon (10)

Dragons, Did They Exist?

Once upon a time, in ancient China, an imaginative little girl named Ping was playing in the forest, not knowing what adventures lay before her ...

Light-headedly, she crossed the river, that nobody else would dare cross, because of the haunted woods that lay on the other side.

Once she reached the woods, Ping was curious and decided to have a look around. However, she lost her footing, consequently she fell through some bushes ...

Ping looked up, not believing her eyes. There, suspended in the air, was a mysterious, magical, illuminating portal. Willingly, Ping jumped in.

Amazingly, she discovered a whole new world - a world of dragons! It was a tropical jungle, nothing like the ones on Earth. Far to the east, there were mountains. In the bushes, there was a baby dragon playing. Ping soon became friends with the optimistic baby. She named him Kai.

From that day on, Ping would visit the dragon world each day but the fun wouldn't last forever.

One day, Ping was playing with Kai when his parents came along and tried to attack her. Fortunately Kai stood up for her. Kai's parents accepted Ping and gave her a tour of Dragon-world. They lived happily ever after.

Isma Saeed (11)

Superdog

I'm going to tell you about a dog who saved the world.

It all started when Jessica and Tom asked if they were allowed a dog. Their parents were so kind, of course they said yes. In no time at all they had a wonderful dog. What they didn't know, was that he was a Superdog. But surprisingly, they called him 'Super'.

One day, Super was playing his favourite game: digging, when suddenly a man appeared before him on a screen. The man said, 'Well Super, I know you're a Superdog. Sorry, I forgot to introduce myself. I'm Mr Evil. Anyway, two hours until the end of the world when this time bomb blows up!'

Super had two hours to save the world. What was he going to do? Well, I'll tell you. He sniffed the air … Suddenly he smelt Mr Evil. He ran as fast as he could to the Evil Office. He saw Mr Evil set the time bomb, then Mr Evil left. Super opened the time bomb but he didn't know which wire to cut because dogs are colour blind. So he sniffed the wire and cut it … Yes it was the right one!

And Superdog is truly super!

Keira Mackey (9)

The Treasure Of Aqua Island

The sea shimmered like diamonds whilst me and my crew sailed to Aqua Island. Noticing a ship in the distance, my heart plummeted. It was a pirate ship! Grabbing my telescope, I realised it was Pirate Putrid.

The ship approached rapidly and Putrid clambered onto my boat. 'I am Pirate Putrid!' he shrieked. 'What are you doing in my sea?'

'We're sailing to Aqua Island,' I said shaking.

'Oh,' the pirate said, happily. 'Me too. I'm seeking the treasure there!'

'We'll find your treasure if you spare our lives,' I said.

Putrid agreed!

I could see the Isle of Aqua, with golden sand, it looked stunning. When we got there everybody began digging and seeing an X. I dug too. My spade hit something. I pulled out a treasure chest and had an idea. 'I've found the chest!' I yelled, later.

Putrid ran to me and wrenched open the chest before screaming. It was empty!

'I think Captain Creep stole the treasure,' I said.

Pirate Putrid looked terrified and sailed away.

'We have the treasure!' I yelled happily. My crew looked confused. 'I hid the treasure! Everybody knows that Putrid's terrified of Captain Creep, so the rest was easy!'

Ellen Ottaviano (12)

Summer Sunshine

There was a little girl called Lilly who loved to surf. She would surf every day in the summer when it was sunny. Lilly would say to her family, 'I'm going to surf in the summer sunshine.' She loved surfing, it was her favourite thing in the world.

One day she went to get her surfboard and couldn't find it anywhere. There was seaweed on the beach, birds in the sky but no surfboard, only her friend's surfboard. She phoned her friend Katie straight away. Katie said that Lilly's surfboard was at her house. Lilly thought this was strange so she walked over to Katie's house and got her surfboard to go surfing.

When she was out in the sea she saw something gliding towards her. It was a pink and blue dolphin with a huge smile.

The dolphin said, 'Sorry I was riding on your surfboards. I just wanted to see which one was the best.'

Lilly said, 'Don't worry about it.'

The dolphin said, 'Will you be my friend?'

Lilly said, 'Yes.'

And from that day on Lilly and the dolphin, whose name turned out to be Bubbles, were the best of friends.

Emily Ewart (7)

The Murder

The pale moon shone through the clouds, feebly lighting the road. The wind blew strongly outside and the rain was plummeting down as if the whole sky was falling in. The shouts of drunken men were loud and harsh in the tavern. Everything was perfectly normal but a certain eerieness crept through the village as if something of terrific horror was about to happen.

No one was outside except a small boy of about nine years of age. His clothes were in tatters and he shivered in the rain - alone, scared and lost. His hair was like mouldy hay, his hands were covered in dirt and as he stumbled along the cobbled streets, with no shoes on his feet, he was completely unaware of the danger that lurked round the corner.

Suddenly a tall hooded figure dressed completely in black emerged out of the alley behind the boy. 'Ello,' he rasped mockingly. 'I've been expecting you.' He drew out a long, razor-sharp blade and raised it high in the air. In an instant he vanished and the boy lay sprawled on the floor, dying in a pool of his own deep red blood.

Dilan Saujani (12)

Burning Flames

Erupting from the bubbling pool of lava was Viscar, the champion of the underworld. Viscar stepped out of the lava and sprinted to the armoury, to prepare for the death match against the lord, Rangoth.

After he arrived at the arena he walked on, hearing claps and cheers as Viscar ignited his bloodthirsty flames. Taking their places in the arena, Viscar sheathed his bloodstained sword. The horn blew! Silence fell! Rangoth charged!

Viscar leapt into the air, dodging the blows of Rangoth's deadly blade. Viscar slammed his fist into the ground, creating an earthquake, sending Rangoth hammering into the crowd. Rangoth clambered back into the arena whilst blood trailed behind him. 'Surrender or I'll make your death even more gruesome than I planned to,' demanded Viscar as he punched Rangoth in the face.

'Never!' screamed Rangoth, letting his voice be heard throughout the entire arena.

Suddenly a flame ignited in Rangoth's chest, tearing his insides apart, sending guts flying everywhere. 'This is just the beginning of what's going to happen to every living thing in Hell,' announced Viscar, as flames ignited all over his body.

Kieran Hall (11)

My Mysterious Adventure

It was very exciting because we were going on holiday which we had planned for a long time. I couldn't sleep.

When we finally reached our destination we made our way out of the aeroplane, through the crowds. I looked back and suddenly realised that my family was not with me anymore. In fact there was hardly anybody there and the car park was all empty. As I walked further, the airport drifted away and all around me there were trees, woods and darkness.

I was calling out for my family and going deeper into the forest. The trees started to lean forward and tried to attack me. I was running and calling for help. There were traps everywhere and very strange creatures came towards me. I was very frightened and suddenly I fell into a very deep, dark hole. When I hit the bottom I suddenly woke up, realising it was only a dream and I was still in the aeroplane.

Our flight had landed. We made our way out. Until we reached our destination, there was only one question in my head … 'Was that a dream or will it really happen?'

Saliha Kauser (8)

My Summertime Story

I was walking along a river one day, looking at all the lovely nature and thinking …

If I could be a butterfly flying all around showing all my bright colours, like the gleaming sun, I would flutter my wings elegantly. My wings would be as delicate as a flower petal. I would be precious, the most precious of all. I would look by the side of the river and watch the humans down below. If I was a butterfly I could smell the fresh air and get the breeze on my face. I could go around the whole world without flying on an aeroplane. I could get everyone's attention using my bright colours that everyone can see. If I was a butterfly I could meet with all my butterfly friends. All the butterflies are different in each and every way. I would watch all the butterflies fly in the sky and say if I could be a butterfly one day.

Amelia Gratton (11)

The Abandoned Cottage

I pushed open the old door and I stepped inside, just before the door creaked shut behind me. I took a deep breath. I was there for a reason; the letter telling me to come was in my pocket. I took it out and read it yet again. It said:

Dear Alice,

You must come to the abandoned cottage on Sunday at midnight. I have something very important and dangerous to tell you.

From?

*I was th*ere and yet there was no one to meet me. I knew I had to be there, the letter had said that but this place was creepy and plus, I thought *I don't even know who's supposed to meet me*. I glanced around the room one more time at the cobwebs and the dusty furniture.

I turned to go when I saw something glowing out of the corner of my eye. A ghost!

Then suddenly I woke up in my bed screaming. I breathed a sigh of relief. It was only a dream. But then I felt something in my pocket. I pulled it out, it was a letter. I read it anxiously, my blood chilled. What was happening? Was it really a dream?

Caitlin Loveys (11)

My Adventure With Batman

Dad decided to move home to Gotham City because he had been offered a good job there and had found a lovely new home.

Batman rescued me from some bullies and he asked me if I could help him to find The Joker. I said, 'Yes, Batman.'

I was allowed to drive the Batmobile, go in the Batcave and have a free Batman costume and cape. It was great fun and so exciting to be with my hero.

We went to the circus to find The Joker, a very nasty and evil criminal. We found him in a dressing room planning to destroy the city. Then Batman had a fight with The Joker, throwing punches, but then he threw a poisonous card at Batman. Batman dodged the card which got stuck in the wall - it had steel tips. Then he threw a couple more cards but Batman dodged them all. Then he said, 'Every good magician always puts an ace up his sleeve,' and he threw the last card at Batman, who dodged it with an enormous somersault leap and then he handcuffed The Joker.

He was sent to jail and shook the bars of the tall door in fury.

Michael Ghose (9)

I Wish I Could Be A Pirate (Not)

Once there was a boy called George who hated school,. he wanted to play all day.

One day there was a fire at school. The fire burnt the school badly so it was closed. There was no other school nearby, so he couldn't go to school. George was delighted. Then his father Bill got a letter informing him that it was going to be rebuilt. The letter said: 'No school until the new school year, yours sincerely, Mr Smith, head teacher.'

'I wish I could be a pirate,' George said to himself. Just at that moment there was a knock at the door. It was Captain Pugwash.

'Would you like to be part of my new crew?' Captain Pugwash exclaimed.

'Yes please,' George shouted.

'Come with me then George,' Captain Pugwash said joyfully. Captain Pugwash then took George back to his ship.

The next day George helped Captain Pugwash. George loved being part of Captain Pugwash's crew until ... it got very dull and boring and everyone except Captain Pugwash was horrible to him. He wished he wasn't a pirate anymore. Then ... Captain Jake stole George from Captain Pugwash.

The next night George swam home.

Emily Ghose (11)

The Daydream

I sat on the swing … backwards, forwards. My face tickled as the wind whistled. My eyes fell closed, enjoying the breeze. Flying above the town, the air rippled my feathers. People bustled around below. Blending green fields, golden corn swaying.

Suddenly the corner of my eye caught movement. A colourful bird swooped up, he could be chasing me! I flapped hard and plunged into a dive.

The ground rushed towards me. The gust seemed to hold me back. A darkness surrounded and cloaked me as I darted through the cold damp air of a cave and shot out into the blinding sunlight. I felt the discomfort of a presence behind me. Buildings loomed ahead. I dodged a wall into a narrow passageway, with one way out I raced in through an open window. The smell of chocolate cake just like my mum makes distracted me as I flew through and open door back into the cool fresh air. Glancing behind, I caught an explosion of glass as a limp form erupted through a window and crumpled. Yes! I'm free … *Thud!* I hit something hard. I opened my eyes. The crisp green grass irritated my face. I'd fallen off the swing.

Frederick Tiso (10)

Pirates

Captain Fishrod spat on his grubby handkerchief and polished his shiny oak leg, pondering as they sailed towards Skullcave Island.

'Land ahoy!'

Fishrod recognised the vessel of his mortal enemy, Deedosovick. Fishrod led the Gory Crew, who crept silently behind, heading for the cave.

Fishrod arrived at the Tunnelly Cave, feeling he'd been followed. They came to the chamber of swords with its concealed entrance. The Gory Crew hid inside and watched as Deedosovick's crew passed by. They were sure to be lost in the cave for days.

Fishrod led his crew through the chamber to another tunnel, which eventually brought them to Hellbone Point. There was a rounded cave with many skeletons scattered on the damp floor. Sitting and resting for a while they mysteriously fell asleep, awaking later to find their precious things had been moved around. Fishrod couldn't stand up, as he had no oak leg. He was very angry to find Hatrib, the cabin boy, holding the oak leg and he had it hottest.

'How dare you take my oak leg? I'll have to polish it all day after your greasy fingers have been on it!' They were all quiet after that.

Annie Tiso (9)

Over The First Branch

Tom always loved climbing his tree, but the problem was he could only climb to the first branch.

One day Tom's friend, Marcus, came round and there was nothing to do. But it was the summer holidays, so they thought about something interesting to do. Marcus was really good at climbing trees, but he knew that Tom could only climb to the first branch. So Marcus asked Tom if he wanted to learn how to climb higher. Guess what Tom said? 'What a super idea! I never thought of that!' and skipped on one leg. Next he shouted, 'Yeahhhhh!'

After, Marcus took Tom to climb the tree.

Then when Tom could climb high, he had an idea and said to Marcus, 'Shall we build a tree house?'

They really started building hard. They worked five days long. It was a fun time. The two friends enjoyed it. Tom didn't realise he'd climbed high and when he realised he was shocked. He was proud of himself.

It was his best holidays ever because Tom discovered he was brave in his heart!

Zofia Czubak (8)

The Mysterious Box

It was a cool summer's night at the docks of Memphis where the stars were out. Chelsea, Tom and John were going to catch the boat to visit their grandma in Thailand.

Chelsea and the twins (Tom and John) were sitting in their seats talking when suddenly … everything went black. The next thing they knew they were floating on a piece of the boat in the middle of nowhere.

'Oh look, there is the shore, it is only a little further, let's just swim,' said Chelsea.

'That was hard work,' said Tom, exhausted.

'Where are we?'

'I don't care, let's explore.'

'Wow, look what I found,' shouted John.

'Let's open it,' said Tom excitedly. Just as they opened it a bright light shot out and they ended up waking on the same island but it was somehow different …

They all looked around and saw animals they thought only existed in their imagination. The twins seemed not to remember anything, whereas Chelsea remembered everything. Confused she grabbed the box and opened it to see if she could set things right.

However she ended up where they were all supposed to be with her grandma in Thailand.

'So where are Tom and John?' asked Chelsea, now really confused.

'Who …?'

Memphis Morey (11)

Stranded

I awoke to a sudden jolt, frightened screams sounded, whilst life jackets were handed out - I feared our time was up.

Leaping out into the ocean tingled my nerves - I couldn't swim. I remained motionless, unable to yell, frozen to the spot, whilst the weakening voice of my mother screamed for me to stay close. The current, stronger now, pulled me from her grasp towards the shore.

Two weeks had passed now, alone on a deserted island, just an empty beach with a small amount of debris, all that remained of our aircraft. A cave offered shelter, whilst water was collected in a metal tin. A bamboo and a hook from a coat hanger provided me with a basic rod.

Loneliness had become my only companion, when a faint noise began to approach. Then, as the clouds were pushed aside by the force hovering in front, my life within its hands, I hesitated before realising, this was my way out. Sprinting across to the cluster of logs exhausted me. Sparks flew as I rubbed the logs frantically, eventually flames rose from the wood.

I climbed into the helicopter, into the arms of my mother, crying and relieved. Reunited.

Leanne Middleton (12)

Young Writers Information

We hope you have enjoyed reading this book - and that you will continue to enjoy it in the coming years.

If you like reading and writing poetry drop us a line, or give us a call, and we'll send you a free information pack.

Alternatively if you would like to order further copies of this book or any of our other titles, then please give us a call or log onto our website at www.youngwriters.co.uk

Young Writers Information
Remus House
Coltsfoot Drive
Peterborough
PE2 9BF
(01733) 890066